Copyright © 2012 Susan Epstein

Premier Publishing & Media
Premier Education Solutions
3839 White Avenue
Eau Claire, Wisconsin 54702

Printed in the United States of America

ISBN: 978-1-936128-11-2

All rights reserved. No part of this book may be reproduced or transmitted in any form or by any means, electronic or mechanical, including photo copying, recording or by any information storage and retrieval system without written permission from the author, except for the inclusion of brief quotations in a review.

Library of Congress Cataloging-in-Publication Data

Epstein, Susan.
　Quick tips for kids / Susan Epstein.
　　　p. cm.
　ISBN-13: 978-1-936128-07-5
　ISBN-10: 1-936128-07-1
　1. Parenting--Psychological aspects. 2. Parent and child.
　3. Learning disabilities--Treatment. I. Title. HQ755.E.E67 2011
　649'.1--dc23
　　　　　　　　　2011024808

Over 60 Techniques, Activities, Worksheets

for Challenging Children & Adolescents

Motivators · Contracts · Homework Strategies · Conversation Starters
Play Therapy · Organization Mindfulness · Self-Esteem · Communication
Skills · Behavioral Change · Personal Growth · Skill Building

Individuals | Groups | Families | Teens

by Susan Epstein, LCSW

Table of Contents

Section 1
Quick Tips for Assessment and Treatment Planning

1. Informed, Involved and On Board — 15
2. Parenting and the System: Case Study — 17
3. What's Really Wrong? — 21
4. Children's Mental Health and Learning Disabilities: What's the Connection? — 23
   Checklist: Red Flag Behaviors in Children and Adolescent

Section 2
Quick Tips to Manage Anger and Explosive Behaviors

Worksheet: Know Thyself: Our Own Childhood/Teenage Years
5. Agenda Circles: An End to Power Struggles — 29
6. Just the Facts: Simplifying Communication — 31
   Worksheet: Formula for Just the Facts
7. It's Not Fair! — 33
8. Birthday Cake! — 35
9. Name It, Don't Blame It! — 37
10. Visual Cue Cards: Ending the Explosions — 39
11. Putting It All Together: Building a Cooling Down Kit — 41

Section 3
Quick Tips for Depressed and Traumatized Children

12. It Looks Like Fun! — 45
13. Big Bird Grows Up — 47
14. Beautiful Bags — 49
15. Blue, Blue — 51
16. Nightmares and Superheroes — 53
17. Bad Things Happen to Great Kids — 55
18. Know Thyself: Helping Children Grieve — 57
19. Parent FAQs About Children and Grief — 59

Section 4
Quick Tips for Depressed and Traumatized Adolescents

20.	Conversation Starters that Engage Even the Most Resistant Teens	65
21.	Sailboats on the Sea: Feeling Focused Art Therapy	67
	Worksheet: Debriefing the Sailboat	
22.	See, Hear, Feel: 5-4-3-2-1	69
23.	Feel the Feeling: The Only Way Out is Through	71
24.	Turning Fear into Courage	73

Section 5
Quick Tips for Kids with ADD and Executive Function Disorder

Checklist: Executive Function Disorder

25.	Any Day Tool Kit	81
26.	Pom-Poms and You	83
27.	Poker Chips for Electronics	85
28.	Whistle While You Work: Taking Care of Our Belongings	87
29.	Give Them a Hook	89
30.	Behavior Charts that Really Work	91

Section 6
Quick Tips to Manage Risky Teenage Behaviors

31.	Difficult Conversations: Parent Guide	97
	Parent Worksheet: Difficult Conversations	
	Sample Parent and Teen Contract:	
	Out with Friends Unsupervised	
32.	Parents as Good Role Models for Teen Drivers	101
	Sample Parent and Teen Contract: Teen Driving	
33.	Parents: What You Need to Know About Your Teen and Drugs and Alcohol	103
34.	Parent Ammo: The Written Word	105
	Write Me an Essay	

Section 7
Quick Tips on How to Command Respect Minus the Fear Factor

35.	Which Behaviors Do You Want to Stop?	**113**
36.	Commanding Respect	**115**
	Setting Up Expectations	
37.	Watch Out for Negativity	**117**
38.	Provide Nurturance and Guidance	**119**
39.	Listen for Feelings	**121**
	Worksheet: Emotional Hot Buttons and Losing It!	
40.	Mindful Robotic Parenting	**123**
	Parent Worksheet: 4-Step Process	

Section 8
Quick Tips for Helping Teens Achieve Their Dreams

41.	Teen's Wheel of Life: Assessment and Tracking	**129**
	Debriefing the Wheel	
42.	Coach a Teen: Getting Started	**133**
	Worksheet: Teen Coaching Check-In	
43.	Dear Best Friend	**135**
	Worksheet: Dear Best Friend	
44.	Visions of Hope: "If You Could Wave a Magic Wand…"	**137**
45.	Dream Boards	**139**
46.	Volunteering: Getting to Thank You!	**141**
	Worksheet: Volunteering Brainstorm	

Section 9
Quick Tips to Manage Homework Hassles

47.	Setting Up a Homework Station	**147**
48.	We All Have Homework	**149**
49.	Be a Helper, Not a Doer	**151**
50.	It's the Effort that Counts	**153**

51. Organize and Chunk Out Homework	**155**
52. Tutors and Mentors	**157**
53. Homework: When It's More Complex	**159**
54. When is the Best Time to Do Homework?	**161**
Parent-Child Homework Agreement	

Section 10
Fostering Independence at Home

55. Which Behaviors Do You Want to Start or See More Of?	**167**
56. The Carrot and the Stick: Why Rewards Sometimes Don't Work	**169**
57. How to Outsource Your Laundry for Free: Life Skills Training	**171**
58. Kids as Cooks	**173**
59. Magic Black Bag: How Not to Trip Over Backpacks, Skateboards, Etc.	**175**
60. Allowance is What You Are Allowed: Early Lessons in Financial Responsibility	**177**
61. Just One More Glass of Water Getting Kids to Bed and Sleeping Through the Night	**179**

Section 11
Quick Tips for Parenting in the New Millennium

62. Blended Families and Discipline: "You're not my dad! You can't tell me what to do!"	**185**
63. Sleep and Obesity: What's the Connection?	**187**
64. Healthy Home Makeover	**189**
65. Technology and Distractibility: Its Affect on Concentration	**191**
66. Enjoying Your Kids While Working from Home	**193**
67. Family Meetings: Run Your Home Like a Business	**195**
68. How to Write a Family Mission Statement	**197**
Worksheet: Family Mission Statement	

Bibliography   **201**

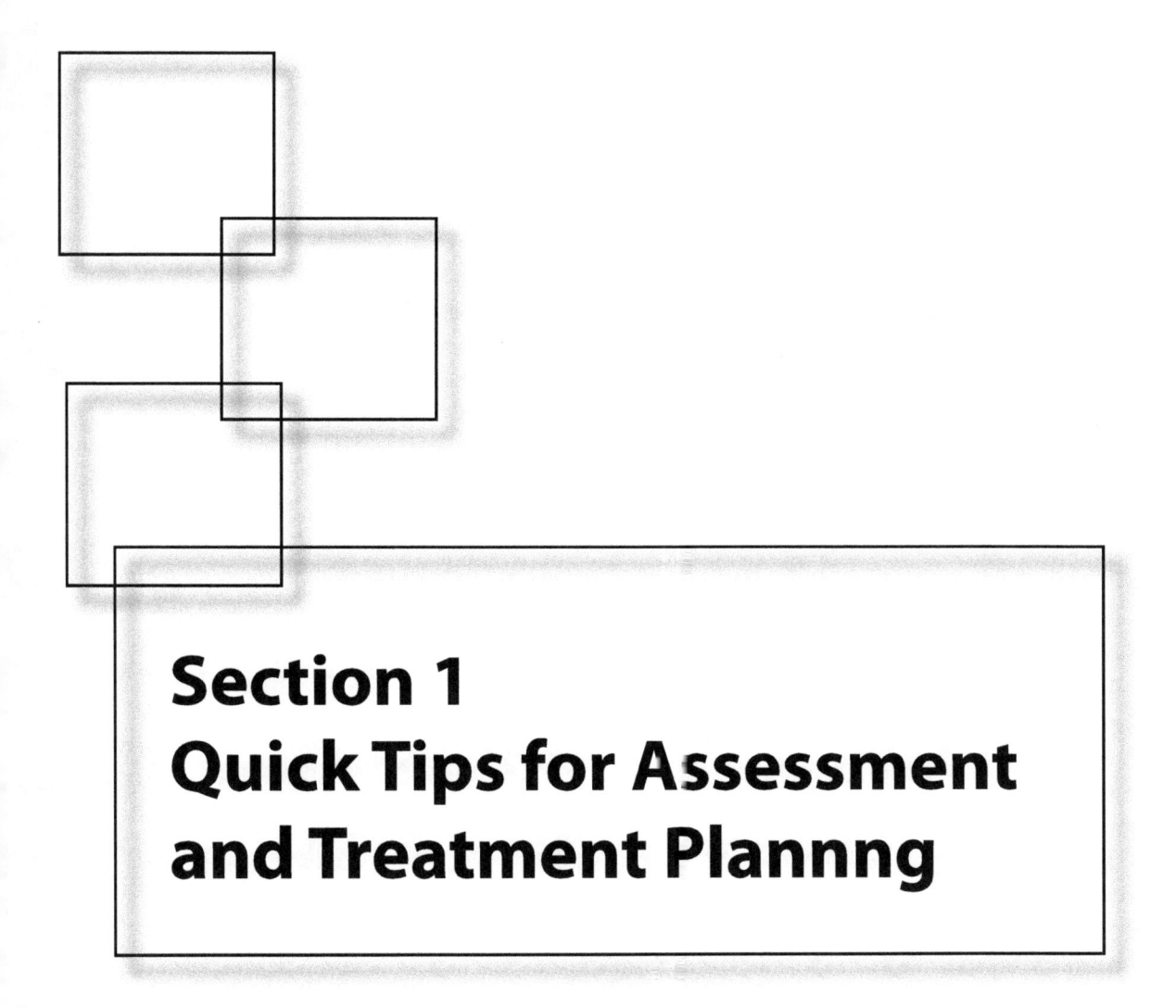

Section 1
Quick Tips for Assessment and Treatment Plannng

Section 1: Quick Tips for Assessment and Treatment Planning

1. Informed, Involved and On Board

Children and adolescents are being diagnosed with mental health labels that may lead to or require psychotropic medications. These include ADD (Attention Deficit Disorder), ADHD (Attention Deficit Disorder Hyperactivity), Bipolar Disorder, ODD (Oppositional Defiant Disorder).

Jenny often interrupts, doesn't listen, doesn't complete tasks, is often obstinate and treats authority figures with little or no respect. At home, parents yell, scream, ground and then do it over again.

It seems like Bobby has come off one grounding only to find himself grounded again. Mom feels like a prison guard and home is hostile and tense. At school, the story repeats.

Johnny is the class clown, constantly talks back to the teacher and serves detention after detention. At the parent/teacher conference the teacher recommends that Johnny get tested for "ADHD" or "other issues." The parent may be relieved; at least his negative behavior has a name! Life is finally going to improve! A psychosocial evaluation is recommended and carried out by the school, now Johnny has a diagnosis. Sometimes, however, this very important step is skipped.

Most state school systems are not permitted to recommend medication. However, they can say, "Talk to your pediatrician" or "Your child needs counseling." Most parents, when given such feedback, will take their child to the pediatrician who will often prescribe or make a referral to a psychiatrist.

His acting out behavior doesn't really change that much with just the medicine, so the psychiatrist refers Billy to a therapist. Once a month his parents or caregiver sit in the waiting room at the psychiatrist's office and every week while the child is seen by the therapist. The most common form of therapy is individual therapy (the 90806-45-50 minute hour).

In the beginning, Billy's parents will see some positive changes in his attitude and behavior and begin to see some progress at home. Billy may seek his parents out more or even treat them respectfully once in a while. We call this the honeymoon period. Parent is driving child to therapy, child is playing or talking with another adult who cares about them, parent is driving child home from the therapy appointment. By nurturing the child, spending alone time with him/her, he/she will naturally respond to this positive attention and his/her behavior will improve.

Then it's over….a phone call to the therapist that Louis was suspended for getting in a fight or Andrew pushed his mother or Melinda hasn't come home for three days.

Challenging Children & Adolescents

What went wrong?

When we medicate the kids for ADD, etc. and then put them in individual therapy when there is the option of family therapy, doing the kids and the parents a great disservice. There are certain situations where parents cannot be involved, such as residential treatment facilities, some foster care situations and some programs. The solution here is to find the person who is the caregiver and involve them.

If a child is disrespectful, acting out, depressed or having other mental health or learning issues it is far more effective to involve the parent/caregiver in the therapy session. Some therapists are constrained by where they work to who they can see. It is up to the therapists to discuss these issues with their supervisors to always do what is in the best interest of the client.

Our world today is more complex, demanding, fast paced and confusing than it was years ago. There are many different kinds of families and many new challenges facing parents than ever before, such as multiple divorce, single parenthood, remarriage, step-parenting, same sex parents, and grandparents raising grandchildren. What your family looks like does not matter. All these arrangements have the potential to raise healthy and happy children. What matters most is that parent figures are informed, involved, and on board.

This book is designed with the intention that therapists and parents/caregivers will be working together. Therapists can use the tips and exercises to model and teach parents how to communicate and discipline effectively. Parents can take the handouts home and follow through on what has been discussed in the family therapy sessions.

Section 1: Quick Tips for Assessment and Treatment Planning

2. Parenting and the System: Case Study

One day Jeffrey came home from school with a chip on his shoulder. His mother, Ellen, asked him what was wrong and Jeffrey went into a tirade like his mother had never seen before. He did have an explosive temper and had punched a hole in the wall in his bedroom last year, but today was different. He started throwing lamps and turning over tables. Ellen hid in the bathroom and called her husband, Rick. Rick called the police who met them at the house. Jeffrey was arrested. Ellen and Rick followed the police car to the station. Jeffrey was fingerprinted and released to his parents with an order to appear in juvenile court the next day. When they returned home, Jeffrey went to his room, Ellen cried herself to sleep, and Rick called a lawyer.

The next day the family appeared in court. Ellen, mortified and ashamed, tried to hide behind a magazine while the family waited for over two hours. Jeffrey appeared sullen and angry and Rick paced. Finally they met with the juvenile probation officer. The probation officer told the parents that Jeffrey needed "anger management." Ellen told the PO that Jeffrey had been in therapy and on meds since he was 5. The probation officer shrugged his shoulders and suggested that the family look around for a residential treatment facility for Jeffrey. Meanwhile, Jeffrey would have to be drug tested once a month at the court. Those were the rules.

How it got to this point…

From the time Jeffrey Miller was two years old he was a handful. Ellen quit her job to stay home with Jeffrey, but she secretly wished that she could go back to her corporate job with all the demands, long hours, commute, etc. because it was a piece of cake next to taking care of her little boy.

Rick was a devoted husband and father, but he had no patience for dealing with Jeffrey's "NOs!" and never-ending tantrums. Jeffrey challenged his parents every chance he got; from throwing temper tantrums in stores if he didn't get a toy or candy to hitting and spitting at his mother when she was trying to dress him, brush his teeth, feed him or put him to bed. Jeffrey's dad would yell "Don't hit your mother!" then give Jeffrey a spank.

Ellen was at a loss and began reading parenting books, magazines and talking to other mothers. Ellen tried time-outs but these turned into day-long battles of will and by the time Jeffrey was 4, Ellen found herself giving in to him just to avoid another battle.

Challenging Children & Adolescents

When it was time for Jeffrey to go to preschool, Ellen was excited because she felt that the reason he was so difficult was because he didn't have other kids to play with on a regular basis. What appeared at first to be a solution, turned into the beginning of a nightmare for Ellen. Jeffrey was asked to leave 3 preschools that first year due to biting and hitting other children and being disrespectful and rude to staff. Each time it was the same scenario: "Maybe you should take him to therapy…he is an angry little boy."

With nowhere to turn and anticipating that kindergarten would be a disaster, Ellen made an appointment to see a child therapist. In the waiting room, Jeffrey started throwing the toys and books and screaming at the top of his lungs. Ellen tried to calm him down but couldn't. Other mothers and fathers gave her glaring and pitying stares. Ellen felt so ashamed. Finally it was Jeffrey's turn and the therapist asked him to come in. He refused clinging to his mother and tore her skirt. The therapist informed Ellen that Jeffrey's problems were too severe and she was making a referral to a psychiatrist. Ellen couldn't believe her ears…her little boy, not yet 5 years old, was being referred to a shrink? Ellen wondered where she had gone wrong; was she a bad mother? Was this something genetic?

The following week Ellen and Rick brought Jeffrey in to see Dr. Wright, the psychiatrist. The doctor said that Jeffrey most likely had ADHD or a conduct disorder. The only way to be sure was to give Jeffrey a trial of medications. The doctor prescribed Ritalin for Jeffrey and then wait and see if his behavior improved. Ellen and Rick were not happy about this. The side effects seemed dangerous and Ellen knew in the back of her head that she had issues and problems of her own that got in the way of her being an effective mother. But they listened to the doctor and gave Jeffrey the pills.

Jeffrey became Dr. Wright's patient and Ellen sat in the waiting room every Tuesday from 4-4:30pm. Their health insurance didn't cover office visits so in one year the visits to the psychiatrists totaled $7200 and the cost of the medications totaled more than $2700. By the time Jeffrey was in the 8th grade, Ellen and Rick had spent over $24,000 on Jeffrey's meds and over $64,500 on visits with Dr. Wright. Even though it was a huge financial strain, both Ellen and Rick would have done anything to help their son and felt that they were doing the right thing. But the funny thing was that Jeffrey wasn't happy. Aside from the absence of tantrums, nothing much had changed over the years. Jeffrey wasn't social and was often cranky and irritable at the end of the day. Ellen and Rick had to walk around on egg shells so as not to upset him. Ellen had been reading books about ADHD and food allergies and was always trying to find the perfect diet that would cure Jeffrey.

Jeffrey was an average student who just got by. He didn't try very hard and lacked motivation and drive. He didn't cause any problems in the classroom, mostly kept to himself, and didn't attract attention. Since the family was embarrassed about his ADHD and the medication, this was never shared with the school personnel. He took a slow release pill every morning which wore off around 4pm.

Section 1: Quick Tips for Assessment and Treatment Planning

What went wrong?
- *No Family Therapy:* Ellen and Rick were not co-parenting and Ellen was afraid of her son's temper.
- *Testing:* No formal testing had been performed on Jeffrey, diagnosis was based on medication outcomes.
- Possible misdiagnosis and years of medication and labeling affected the entire family system's view of themselves.
- *No Team:* Parents/clinician/school were not working together to help Jeffrey reach his potential, academically and socially.

Jeffrey didn't need to be arrested because his outbursts were a result of misdiagnosis and issues of medication management. The day of Jeffrey's arrest he had rebounded from the ADHD medication going out of his system at the end of the day. Jeffrey didn't need to be arrested (it wasn't his fault or Ellen's or Rick's…they were all following Dr's orders).

Many families dread the evenings when their children's meds wear off. Parents are often not told of all the possible side effects of medications and a situation like this can be very frightening, dangerous and misunderstood. Parents spend thousands and thousands of dollars on therapy, medications and special diets that don't work. In their case, the medications made Jeffrey socially numb, isolated, depressed and explosive.

Section 1: Quick Tips for Assessment and Treatment Planning

3. What's Really Wrong?
Guest Contributor, Mindy Mazur, MPH, Educational Therapist

Children don't live in their own apartments, they live with their families. That's why it's so important that all the helping adults involved try to understand what impact a "bad" kid's behavior has on their family. Teacher, therapist, and parent all want the same outcome for the child, to be successful and confident. How each adult perceives or addresses the situation will probably be very different.

Many parents have noticed the following:
- Child has difficulty learning
- Child's behavior at home and at school is extremely difficult to manage
- Child has had numerous suspensions

Parents may have asked themselves the following questions:
- Is my child's behavior just a phase?
- Can my child's school help us?
- Should my child see a professional? Which kind of professional?
  - And what can they do?
  - How do I find one I know is good?
- What other services are out there?

- Does the child already have an Individualized Education Program (IEP) is on medications like Ritalin, Adderall, and other stimulants with little or no effect?

- Has the school not implemented or followed through with your child's approved program and your child is becoming more depressed and out of control?

- Has the child begun to isolate from friends and family? Is the child smoking marijuana or drinking? Or might they be engaged in other risky anti-social behavior? Or are they already involved in the juvenile justice system?

Tips for getting started:

1. Don't wait to take action.
   - Don't think a child will grow out of their difficulties
   - Don't wait until the end of the next semester to revisit the issue
   - Three months, six months, or one year is a significant amount of time to let pass in a child's education

Challenging Children & Adolescents

2. Meet with the child's teacher immediately.
   - Do not wait for parent/teacher conferences to raise concerns
   - Don't accept the teacher's recommendations to wait until the end of the semester or that the child will grow out of it

3. Have the child's vision and hearing screened.
   - Oftentimes, a child's learning difficulties can be caused by a hearing or visual impairment

4. Request an evaluation.
   - Schools will provide an "Initial Psychological-Educational Evaluation" at their expense, which can give a baseline on your child's cognitive ability, academic achievement, and emotional health

5. Schedule a neuropsychological evaluation.
   - Check with the pediatrician to get a referral, there is often a long wait for an appointment

Section 1: Quick Tips for Assessment and Treatment Planning

4. Children's Mental Health and Learning Disabilities: What's the Connection?
Guest Contributor, Mindy Mazur, MPH, Educational Therapist

Most children are not born with a mental health diagnosis. Often it can be caused by environmental problems, such as trauma, abuse or violence. Emotional difficulties can also arise when a learning disability is present. The interaction between mental health and learning disabilities is complex and not always clear. Here are five main ways in which emotional problems and learning disabilities can interact:

1. Learning disabilities may lead to emotional distress.
2. Learning disabilities may raise or exacerbate existing emotional concerns.
3. Emotional issues may mask a child's learning disability.
4. Emotional issues may exacerbate learning disabilities.
5. Conversely, emotional health may enhance the performance of children with learning disabilities.

What to look for to determine if the child is experiencing emotional difficulties and needs professional help:

- Decline in school performance
- Poor grades despite strong efforts
- Constant worry or anxiety
- Repeated refusal to go to school or to take part in normal activities
- Hyperactivity or fidgeting
- Persistent nightmares
- Continuous or frequent aggression or "acting out"
- Continuous or frequent rebellion and/or temper tantrums
- Depression, sadness, or irritability

Mental health conditions, just like physical illnesses (such as asthma and diabetes), are experienced differently by each child. So remember, **a "diagnosis" does not define the child.** Each student needs their own individualized treatment plan, educational program, and accommodation strategy.

Teachers and clinicians try not to rush to judgment and assume that all they have to do is set limits with their child to rectify the problem. Parents have already tried every possible trick in the book without any success. They may feel ashamed and hopeless. Instead offer support and brainstorm together to uncover possible strategies to help the child.

Checklist: Red Flag Behaviors in Children and Adolescent

____ Secrecy (sneaking around, breaking rules, using drugs/alcohol)

____ Frustration (with communication school, peer and family relationships)

____ Shame (being different, feeling that they are not living up to potential)

____ Depression (clinical and/or situational)

____ Sadness (loss, trauma, loneliness)

____ Boredom (lack of interest and direction, missing opportunities, lacking guidance)

____ Perfectionism (having to be perfect or the best at everything)

____ Lack of clear sense of values or perspective (no structure at home/family, rituals)

____ Isolating (because of appearance, weight, acne, different from peers)

____ Skipping school (fear of failure)

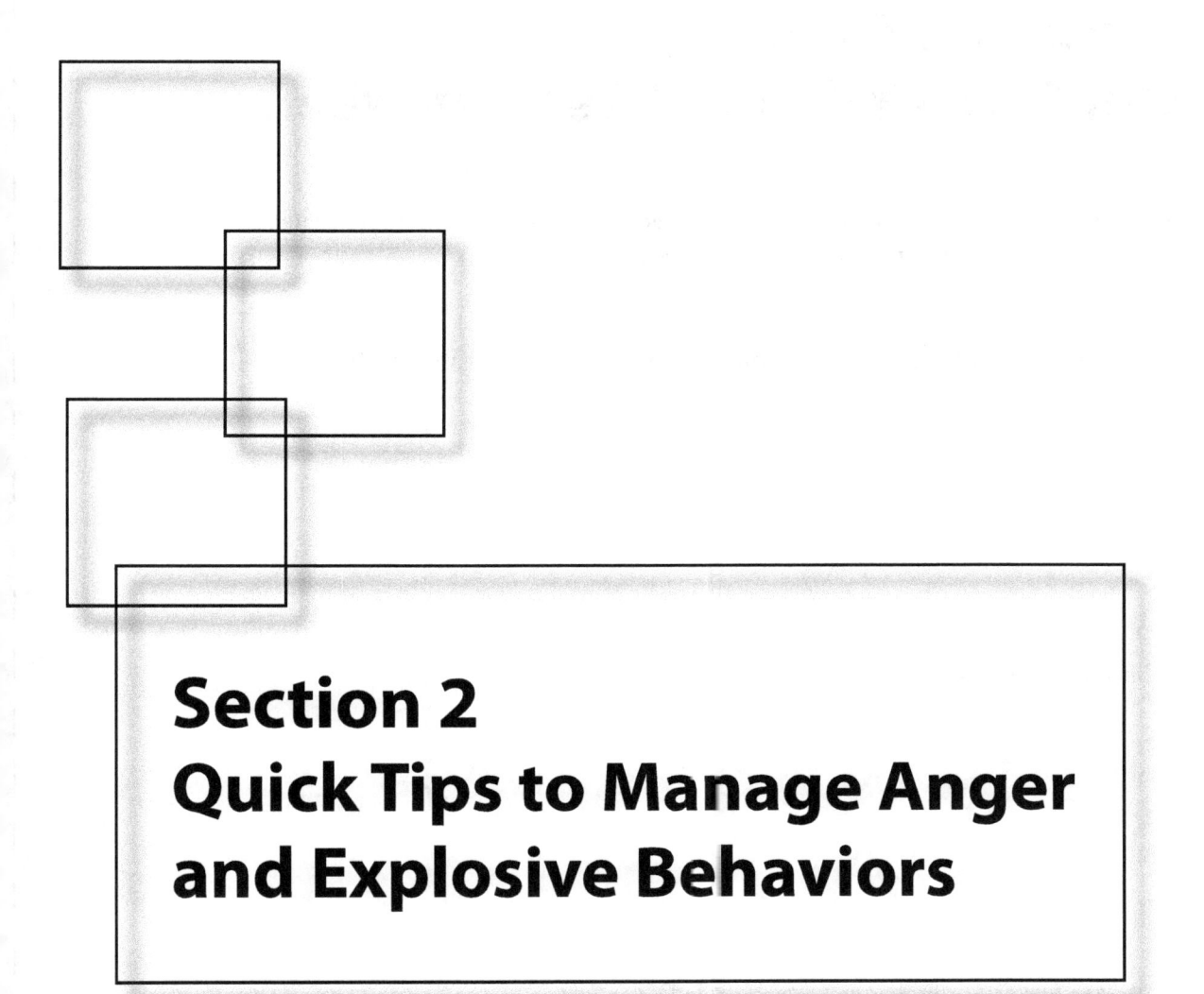

Section 2
Quick Tips to Manage Anger and Explosive Behaviors

Worksheet: Know Thyself: Our Own Childhood/Teenage Years

Whether, parent, therapist, or teacher, it's always a good idea to check in with our own experiences and triggers. Use this form to stay in check with yourself.

When you were a child/teen, what do you remember about anger in your home?

How did your parent(s) handle anger/emotion?

How did you feel about how anger was handled?

How do you handle anger and frustration now?

Section 2: Quick Tips to Manage Anger and Explosive Behaviors

5. Agenda Circles: An End to Power Struggles

Ages: All

Purpose:
To relieve frustration in the communication between parent and child can be frustrating.

Instructions: Drawing a picture can help both parent and child see the other person's point of view. Use the agenda circle handout on the next page to help parents and kids communicate from a place of their own agendas. Then bring them through a conversation where both parties get their needs met. Have parent and child/teen fill in the circles on the next page.

Example:

First Circle: The parent wants the child to clean up his room.

Second Circle: The child wants to watch T.V.

Third Circle: If Jack makes his bed and picks up his towels he gets 30 minutes of TV. (Allows for a plan of how parent and child can both get what they want.)

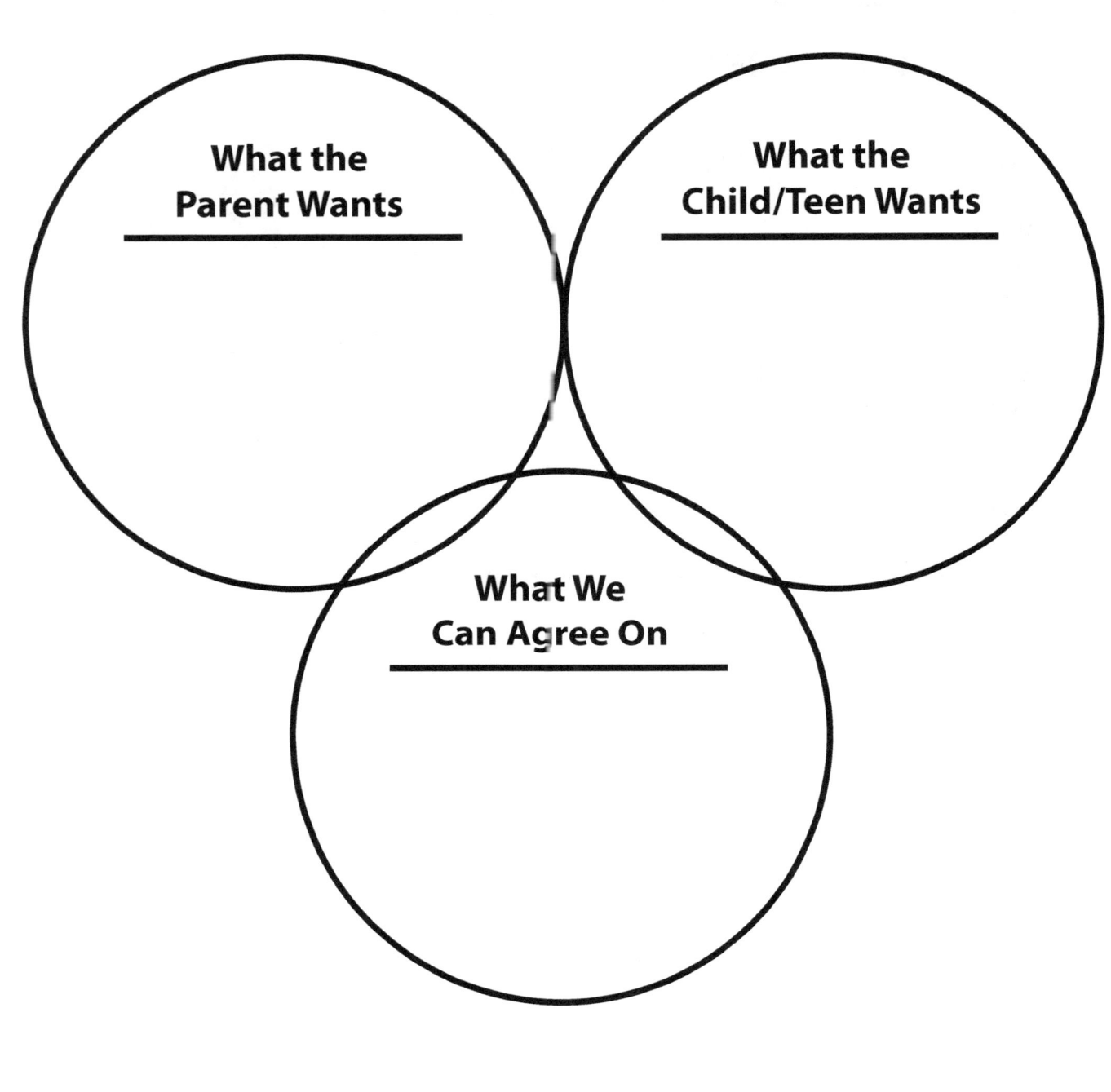

Section 2: Quick Tips to Manage Anger and Explosive Behaviors

6. Just the Facts: Simplifying Communication

Usual Scenario:

Parent: "I can't believe you left your towel on the bathroom floor again. How many times have I told you to hang it up when you are done? Get in that bathroom right now and hang it up!"

Result:

Child/Teen: "Get off my back! Leave me alone! You pick it up if it is bothering you so much!"

Ages: All

Purpose: To get kids to cooperate without tantrums, meltdowns and explosions. Script helps parents remain calm.

Instructions:

Be Calm, Clear & Concise:

"Your towel is on the bathroom floor."

"I feel frustrated because I've asked you to hang it up many times."

"Please hang up the towels when you are done….."

Worksheet: Formula for Just the Facts

State the facts:

_____

_____

_____

_____

How do you feel?

_____

_____

_____

_____

Make a polite request:

_____

_____

_____

_____

Section 2: Quick Tips to Manage Anger and Explosive Behaviors

7. It's Not Fair!

Difficult, challenging and explosive kids believe that the things that happen to them during the course of their day are "unfair." They have a distorted view of "reasonable expectations and demands" from parents, teachers and other authority figures and see these as "unfair."

Ages: 6-13

Purpose: To untangle what children perceive as fair opposed to what they *want* or *don't want* to do.

Materials:

- 3 x 5 index cards
- Pen/pencil/marker

Instructions:

- Make a set of cards to have on hand with the following words:
    1. *Complete homework*
    2. *Do chores*
    3. *Go to bed at bedtime*
    4. *Take a shower*

- Add a few hypothetical situations such as:
    1. *You are playing cards and your friend takes two turns in a row.*
    2. *The teacher passes out cookies and everyone gets 2 but you only get 1.*

- Ask them the difference between the things they are asked to do and unfair requests.

- Now ask the child/teen to talk about the things in his or her life that upset them and create a card for each one.

- Next ask the child/teen to tell you which pile each of their cards belongs in.
    1. *"Unfair"*
    2. *"Just something I don't want to do".*

Section 2: Quick Tips to Manage Anger and Explosive Behaviors

8. Birthday Cake!

Ages: 5-12

Purpose: To teach young children how to self regulate emotions, calm themselves, and relax.

Instructions: Read the following script aloud to the child. Make a recording of the script, then share it with the parent or create a copy for the child to take home.

- Get ready to relax. You can sit in a chair, on the floor or lie down on a bed.
- Close your eyes and pretend you are blowing the candles out on your birthday cake. Oh, no…the candles won't go out! Now you are all out of air, take a big breath in and blow your candles out again. The candles won't go out, they are those trick candles, but you keep trying. Breathe in and then blow out the candles…Keep breathing slowly like this. Feel how it relaxes you to breathe deeply. Finally you are able to blow out all the candles on your cake.
- Now squeeze your hands closed into fists. Pretend that you are squeezing a lemon in each hand…gripping tighter…squeeze even tighter…squeeze all the juice right out of those lemons. Right now, your muscles are tense.
- And now relax. Let your hands go limp. Now your hands feel relaxed. Notice how relaxed your hands feel. Notice how tense feels different from relaxed. Relaxation is a way to make your whole body feel at ease like your hands are now.
- One way to relax your body is by breathing deeply. Imagine that your body is like a balloon. When you breathe in, feel your chest and sides expanding, like a balloon filling with air. When you breathe out, imagine your body is like a balloon shrinking with the air being let out.
- Breathe in like a balloon being blown up. Now breathe out, like the air is being slowly let out of a balloon. Let the air out by blowing the air through your mouth.
- Breathe in through your nose, imagine your body expanding like a balloon and now imagine letting the end of the balloon go, and the air rushing out as you breathe out through your mouth.
- As you breathe in this time, raise your arms above your head. When you breathe out, lower your arms.
- Breathe in. Reach your hands above your head, stretching high up… stretching… and now lower your arms to your sides and relax. Breathe out.
- Raise your arms and breathe in…lower your arms and breathe out…
- Raise your arms and breathe in…lower your arms and breathe out…

Challenging Children & Adolescents

- Now relax and keep your arms at your sides, while you continue breathing slowly and deeply.
- Remember the difference between tense and relaxed. Tighten your leg muscles to make both of your legs tense. Pretend you are riding your bike up a very steep hill and you have to squeeze your legs together and utilize all your power to get to the top of the hill. Squeeze tighter...tighter...and now relax.
- Let your legs become very relaxed. Each leg is as loose as a piece of string.
- Your legs feel heavy. The muscles are loose.
- Now tense your arms. Make the muscles very tight and tense. Tighter...and now relax. Your arms are relaxed, limp and loose as pieces of string.
- Notice how it feels to be relaxed. Your legs and arms are relaxed.
- Now let your whole body become relaxed. Notice how relaxed you can make your body...loosening every muscle...no tension at all...
- Your body feels heavy and relaxed.
- Relax even more by noticing your breathing again. Notice how calm your breathing is. In...out...in...out...
- Keep breathing and simply relax. There is nothing you need to do right now except relax quietly. (pause)

Section 2: Quick Tips to Manage Anger and Explosive Behaviors

9. Name It, Don't Blame It!

Ages: All

Purpose: To diffuse an explosive child or teen.

Instructions:

1. **Stay calm:** Imagine you are a robot in a science fiction film and you are up for an academy award. You cannot show emotion in the film or you will not be nominated.

2. **No lecture:** Lectures put kids into the zone of tuning out. All they hear is blah, blah, blah. They also feel shamed which, we learned before, can lead to explosive outbursts.

3. **No questions:** Questions put kids on the defensive and they feel backed into a corner. This will provoke them to lash out and become very angry.

4. **Be clear:** Don't go on and on. Use as few words as possible to make your point. Children/teens will tune out after as few as 5 words.

5. **Name the behavior:**
   Example: "Please remove your hand from your hip."
   "Please don't roll your eyes, that is disrespectful."

6. **Don't give up until the child/teen stops:** Every time the child/teen comes back with another remark repeat what you just said.

   Example: "Please don't speak to me that way, it is disrespectful."

7. **Do not banish:** Don't send the child/teen to their room. This sends out the signal that you don't care and/or can't stand them.

8. **Follow:** If the child/teen walks away from you, call them back and if they still leave follow while continuing to repeat "I know you are upset, it's okay to take some time, but please tell me that is what you are doing before you walk away."

9. **Visual Reminders:** Use sticky notes, screen savers, etc. to remind yourself to stay calm. "I am a calm parent/teacher and I get results."

10. **Correct with love and guidance:** Show that you care by hanging in there and not losing it, use please and thank you when correcting behavior.

Section 2: Quick Tips to Manage Anger and Explosive Behaviors

10. Visual Cue Cards: Ending the Explosions

Ages: 9-18

Purpose: To teach children and teens how they can turn habitual negative reactions, situations, and feelings into thoughtful and mindful responses.

Materials:

- (4) card stock
- 3 x 5 index cards
- Large sticky notes
- Markers

Instructions: Instruct the child/teen to decorate four cards with the words:

STOP
BREATHE
REFLECT
CHOOSE

On the back of the **STOP** card, write:

- What am I feeling?
- Where am I feeling it in my body?
- It is okay to feel this feeling.

On the back of the **BREATHE** card, write:

- Breathe in and out slowly 5 times and notice the breath.
- Repeat: "I am okay."

On the back of the **REFLECT** card, write:

- How did I react last time?
- How far back can I remember reacting that way?
- Who can I turn to for support?

Challenging Children & Adolescents

On the back of the **CHOOSE** card, write:

- What are my choices/options?
- What is my best choice?
- Choose that now.

Go over the questions with the child/teen and help them brainstorm answers to the options/choices/questions and add those answers to the cards. Allow children/teens to keep these cards to remind them that they can choose how to react.

Section 2: Quick Tips to Manage Anger and Explosive Behaviors

11. Putting It All Together: Building a Cooling Down Kit

Ages: All

Purpose: To calm down, self-regulate emotions, and reduce parent-child conflict.

Materials:

- Bag, shoe box, mini knapsack, Tupperware container, etc.
- All or some of the following: Calming cards, crayons, play dough or model magic (see Blue, Blue #15), small pad of paper, CD with relaxation script (see Birthday Cake #8 and Sailboats on the Sea #21)

Instructions:

Once you have taught the child and parent all the different cooling down techniques, celebrate by creating a container for them to be kept in. Depending on the environment, you can help the family create multiple kits, for home, school, grandma's and even daycare.

The parent or caregiver's role is to prompt and remind the child to use the kit when the child begins to appear agitated. Sit with the child and assist in the cooling down time. So much better than a time out!

Bonus Tip on Breathing:

Have a cotton ball race with the child. "Who can use the straw to blow their cotton ball across the table/floor first?"

Or…use bubbles. "Let's see who can blow the biggest bubble without popping it."

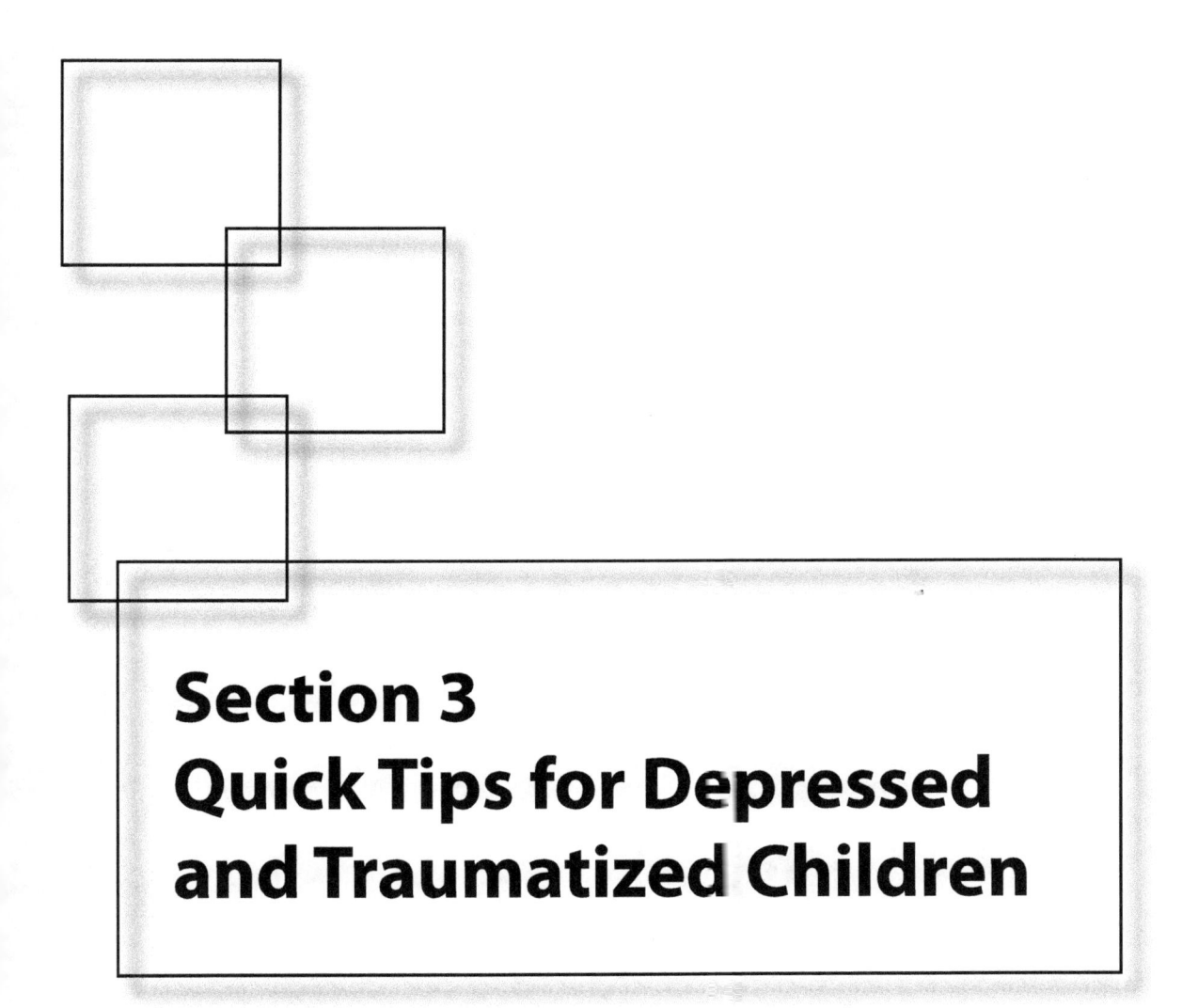

Section 3
Quick Tips for Depressed and Traumatized Children

Section 3: Quick Tips for Depressed and Traumatized Children

12. It Looks Like Fun!

Ages: 4-9

Purpose: To help interaction with the child who won't play or engage with you.

Materials:

- Paper
- Markers

Instructions:

- Get out a piece of paper and a marker and start to draw a picture by yourself.

- Lean over the picture to hide your work. Children are naturally curious and the child will most likely try to see what you are doing.

- Don't let him or her see what you are doing at first.

- Then say tentatively, "Okay…you can watch."

- Continue drawing for a few more minutes.

- Then ask the child if they would like to help you finish the picture.

Section 3: Quick Tips for Depressed and Traumatized Children

13. Big Bird Grows Up

The most frustrating experience for therapists and clients is when no one talks. This is very uncomfortable and often therapists find themselves standing on their heads to get kids to open up. I developed this technique when working with a selective-mute 9-year-old girl.

Ages: All

Purpose: To connect with a resistant, non-talkative or selective-mute child/teen.

Materials:

- Yellow sticky notes
- Pens

Instructions:

Start a conversation on a sticky note. Then stick the note on the child/teen's arm. Hand the sticky notes to the child/teen. They will answer your question and then stick the note on you. See how many stickynotes you can generate. Usually, this will create some laughter and giggles as the sticky notes cover your bodies and you both begin to resemble Big Bird.

Section 3: Quick Tips for Depressed and Traumatized Children

14. Beautiful Bags

Ages: 5-18

Purpose: Engaging with a resistant or non-talkative child or teen in a structured, fun, non-threatening way. This exercise teaches children and teens that therapy can be fun and purposeful while taking the heaviness out of the therapy session.

Materials:

- Paper bag
- Stickers, glitter, glue stick, etc.
- Markers
- Sticky notes or small pieces of paper
- Timer

Instructions:

Session #1: Give the child/teen the craft supplies and the paper bag and say: "Today you get to just create. This is your bag to decorate. I'll tell you later how we are going to use this in our work together." (The therapist keeps the bag at the end of the session.)

Session #2: Explain that you and the child/teen are going to play a game using a timer.

> Possible ideas:
> - "In the next sixty seconds, I want you to say as fast as you can all the things that upset you, no matter what they are."
>   (As the child/teen starts naming these, the therapist writes each one down on a sticky note or small piece of paper and throws it into the bag.)
>
> - "In the next sixty seconds, I want you to say as fast as you can all the different worries or fears that you have."
>   (As the child/teen starts naming these, the therapist writes each one down on a sticky note or small piece of paper and throws it into the bag.)

Challenging Children & Adolescents

Session #3: The therapist instructs the child/teen to close their eyes and pull out one of the slips of paper…and that is what you talk about that session.

Each week, another slip is pulled until all the issues are discussed.

Some kids will respond to some of the slips of paper with "I'm good with that now…but I want to talk about this instead." Abandoning the bag is okay, it was just used to get started. Other kids will ask if they can add more to the bag; also, okay!

Section 3: Quick Tips for Depressed and Traumatized Children

15. Blue, Blue

Ages: 3-9

Purpose: To help young children express feelings. By putting words and colors to feelings it helps to foster appropriate expression of emotions.

Materials:

- Three crayons or markers:
  - Blue = Sad
  - Red = Mad
  - Yellow = Glad
- Pad of paper
- Jar or basket

Instructions:

- Teach children the association between the color and the feeling.

- Keep the 3 crayons/markers and paper in the jar/basket in an easily accessible place in the child's home.

- When they act out, send them to make a picture: "Show me how you are feeling with the colors."

- After school is also a great time: "Show me with the colors how much sad, mad and glad you had today at school."

*For the younger kids, hold the crayons and ask them to point to the one that they are currently feeling. Then ask them to make a picture with that crayon.

Section 3: Quick Tips for Depressed and Traumatized Children

16. Nightmares and Superheroes

Ages: 3-9

Purpose: To help children who have disturbing dreams and sometimes have difficulty falling asleep or staying in their own beds take control of their fear and sleep through the night.

Materials:

- Paper
- Markers
- Crayons
- Glitter

Instructions:

- Ask the child to tell you about the dream/nightmare and draw a picture of the nightmare.
- Now tell the child to tear up the drawing.
- Ask them to create an alternate ending or to create a superhero to come in and save the day. In other words, rewrite the nightmare.
- Have the child draw a picture of the "new dream."
- Discuss how this new dream is going to protect them from the scary nightmare.
- Hang the picture above their bed and talk about it before bedtime.

Section 3: Quick Tips for Depressed and Traumatized Children

17. Bad Things Happen to Great Kids

Ages: 5-12

Purpose: To reduce the stigma of trauma with the reminder and knowledge that other kids have had similar experiences. By rearranging the list from bad to worse, kids gain a sense of control, power and hope.

Materials:

- Paper
- Pen/pencil
- Scissors

Instructions:

- Explain to the child that you are going to make a list together of all the terrible things that can happen to children.
- Take turns saying these things out loud while the adult (therapist/parent) creates the list (if the child is a non-reader pictures can be drawn).
- Some things that could come up:
    - Being teased/bullied
    - Parent dying
    - Parent in jail
    - Sexual/physical abuse
    (Throw some outrageous ones in too, such as "being eaten by a lion")
- Now ask the child to cut the paper into strips so that each terrible thing is its own piece of paper.
- Instruct the child to put the strips in order from bad to worse. Then discuss the order with the child, sorting out the inconsistencies and discussing the reasons why the child ordered them in that particular way.

Section 3: Quick Tips for Depressed and Traumatized Children

18. Know Thyself: Helping Children Grieve

Coping with a death in the family is one of the most difficult challenges that you and your children will ever undertake. Before you begin explaining death to your child, it may be very helpful to look back at your own childhood experiences with death.

Did anyone talk to you about death?

What did they tell you about death?

Do you have stories or experiences with death that you have never spoken about?

Do you remember what you were told about what happens when someone dies?

Because of their own past experiences and fears some parents think they need to protect their children from dealing with death. Most parents are fairly confused and turn to professionals to deal with death and loss; however, you can talk to your own children about death.

Section 3: Quick Tips for Depressed and Traumatized Children

19. Parent FAQs About Children and Grief

1. How do I explain death to a young child?

Tell your child the truth and answer your child's questions. Go to the library and check out children's books on death and read them to your child. "Grandma was sick and her body couldn't work anymore" or "John's dad was killed in a car crash."

2. What words should I use to describe death to my child?

Use language they can understand. Be careful not to use the words "went away," "passed," "lost," etc. Young children will take you very literally and want to know why the loved one has not returned or will want to go look for them.

3. How much information should I share with my child?

Use common sense for how much information you need to share based on the developmental stage of your child. Keep it simple; for example, "Grandpa got sick and his heart stopped working. When someone is very old, their heart isn't as strong."

4. Should I bring my child to the funeral or service?

If your child can sit through a service without you having to entertain him/her or having to get up and take him or her out, s/he can go to the funeral. Being with family members is natural. Seeing people cry at a service is normal, too. It is okay for your child to see this. "Everyone is very sad, and they will miss Grandpa very much, that is why they are crying."

Challenging Children & Adolescents

5. Should I let my child see me cry?

Grieve in front of your child. Do not hide your sadness; instead, show it is okay to cry when someone dies. Also demonstrate how you can deal with your sadness. Look at pictures of happier times together with your child. Ask your child to draw a picture of a favorite time with the loved one that has died.

6. What should I say when my child sees me sad?

Your child will ask you if you are sad. Answer simply, "Yes, I am sad because I loved Grandpa very much and I will miss him."

7. How do I keep the memories alive of the loved one who has died?

Talk with your child about the experiences that they had with the loved one. Look at photos together and make it okay to bring up the loved one's name.

8. What if my child thinks that I will also die?

Explain to your child that that is not likely—but be careful. "We all will die. We just don't know when. Most people live a long life."

9. How do I know if my child is grieving in the "right way"?

There is no right way to grieve. Every child will grieve differently. And there is no length of time when your child should be "done" or "over it." It is a process and grief needs to run its course. Sometimes parents are so overwhelmed themselves in grieving that they would benefit from some help and guidance from a therapist or support group.

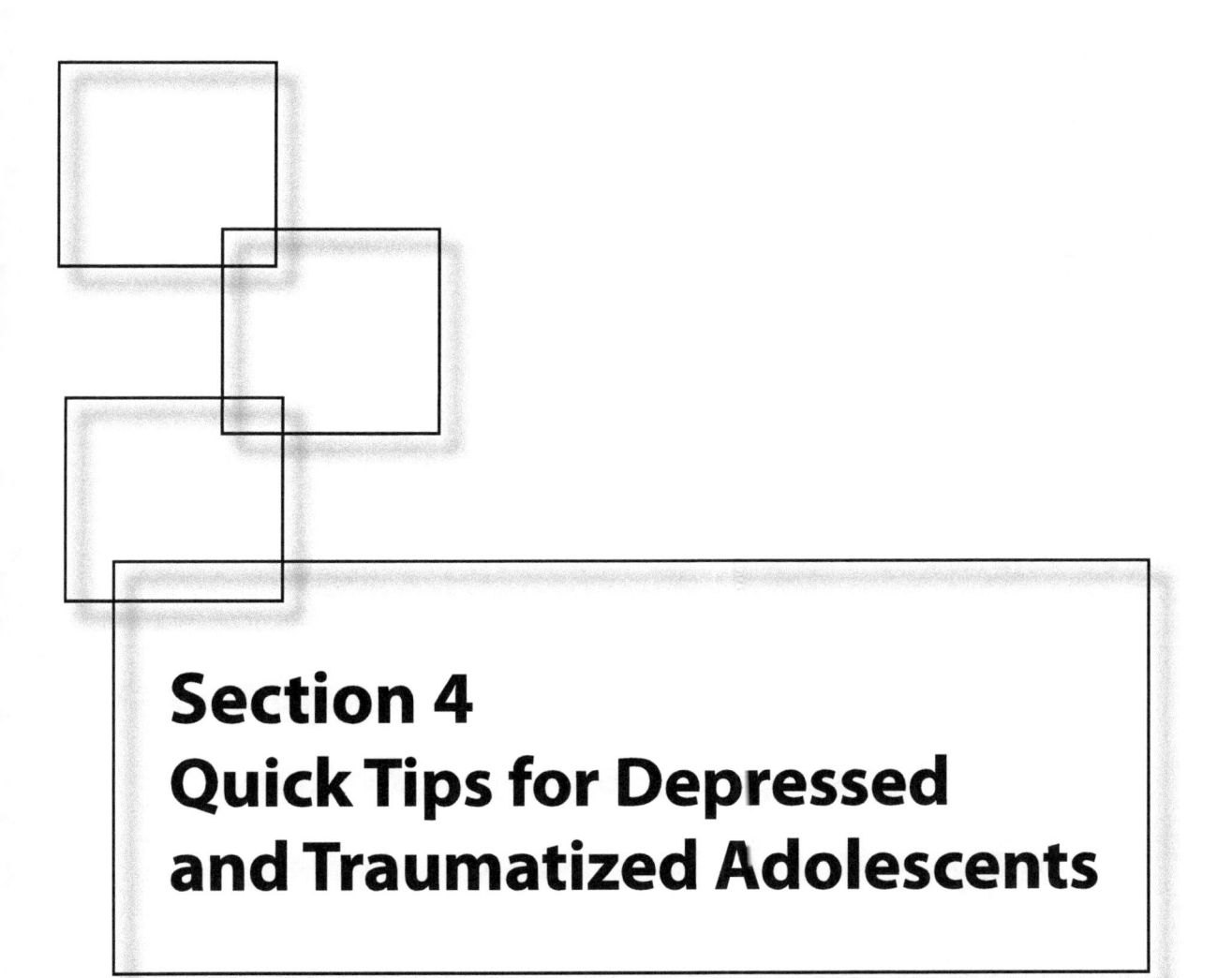

Section 4
Quick Tips for Depressed and Traumatized Adolescents

Section 4: Quick Tips for Depressed and Traumatized Adolescents

20. Conversation Starters that Engage Even the Most Resistant Kids

Ages: 13-18

Purpose: To help you when you are at a loss for what to say.

Instructions:

Open with one of the following to help spark conversation:

- Praise the child/teen: "I really liked the way…"
    (Builds self-esteem)

- "What was the best part of your day?"
    (Shows interest in their lives/encourages verbal expression/connection)

- "What's your plan for the day/evening?"
    (Encourages strategic and realistic thinking)

- "What worked last time you had this problem/issue?"
    (Encourages reflective thinking)

- "If you could do it again, how would you do it differently?"
    (Encourages learning and applying changes)

Section 4: Quick Tips for Depressed and Traumatized Adolescents

21. Sailboats on the Sea: Feeling Focused Art Therapy

Ages: 13-18

Purpose: To unravel and take care of unresolved feelings and emotions. Starts out non-verbal and allows for de-briefing (see worksheet on next page).

Materials:

- Modeling clay or play dough
- Markers
- Paper

Instructions:

- Give client the art materials.
- Read aloud to client the following script:

While sitting in a chair or on the floor…
Close your eyes, and take a deep breath in…now breathe out.
Breathe in…and breathe out again.
Keep breathing slowly like this.
Notice your breath and follow it as it goes in and out of your body.
Now imagine that you are sitting on a peaceful beach in the warm sun, listening to the waves hit the shore.
Ask yourself, "Is there something in the way of feeling good?"
Put your answer on a paper boat and send it out to sea.
Ask the question again, "Is there something in the way of feeling good?"
And put that answer out to sea as well.
Continue asking the question and putting the answers on the boats until there is nothing left to get in the way of feeling okay.
When nothing else comes to mind, check in with yourself one more time.
"Am I completely okay, right now?"
Now, ask yourself this question, "How do I feel most of the time?" Maybe it is worried, scared, or mad…and send that answer out to sea as well.
Now put your attention out to sea and look at all your little paper boats bobbing up and down. See all the things that have been getting in your way of feeling okay.
Pick one that needs your attention right now and pluck that boat out of the water.
When you are ready, gently open your eyes and create an image with the clay or draw out on paper that thing which needs your attention.

Debriefing the Sailboat

1. Once you have taken care of _____, what will that do for you?

2. What would be the best part about that?

3. What do you think might get in the way of taking care of this?

4. What else?

5. What's the worst part about _____?

6. Anything else?

7. What is one small step that you could take right away to begin to take care of _____?

8. Now make another image with the clay or draw a picture representing the next step you will take.

Section 4: Quick Tips for Depressed and Traumatized Adolescents

22. See, Hear, Feel: 5-4-3-2-1

Ages: 13-18

Purpose: To help manage anxiety, flashbacks, nightmares, sleep disturbances, grounding and deep relaxation.

Instructions:

Model the following script first aloud and then have the teen practice on their own aloud with you listening. You can restart and repeat until relaxed. If you or the teen becomes sleepy or drifty…good, that is really the goal…that signals relaxation and it is okay to stop!

> **Name 5 objects you see in the room, one at a time.**
> **Example:**
> I see the chair.
> I see the carpet.
> I see pens.
> I see books.
> I see the door.
>
> **Name 5 sounds you hear.**
> **Example:**
> I hear footsteps.
> I hear the fan.
> I hear a bird.
> I hear a car horn.
> I hear my breathing.
>
> **Name 5 feelings you are having right now.**
> **Example:**
> I feel tired.
> I feel warm.
> I feel anxious.
> I feel excited.
> I feel sad.
>
> **Next:** Name 4 objects you see, 4 sounds you hear, and 4 things you feel.
> **Next:** Name 3 objects you see, 3 sounds you hear, and 3 things you feel.
> **Next:** Name 2 objects you see, 2 sounds you hear, and 2 things you feel.
> **Next:** Name 1 object you see, 1 sound you hear, and 1 thing you feel.

Section 4: Quick Tips for Depressed and Traumatized Adolescents

23. Feel the Feeling: The Only Way Out is Through

Ages: 13-18

Purpose: To reduce panic, anxiety and irrational fears.

Instructions:

Talk the teen through the following script:

What are you feeling in your body?
Where are you feeling it?
Describe what this feels like, looks like. What color is the feeling? How big or small?
I want you to focus on the feeling and stay with it
If you can, close your eyes and keep feeling it.
Tell me when and if the feeling gets stronger, lessens, or moves to another part of your body.
Now I want you to take this feeling in your arms and rock it, give it all the love you can.
Stay with it if you can.

Keep repeating until the feeling significantly lessens or disappears.
Then ask the teen if they can try and feel the feeling again (re-check).

Show the teen that this is something they can do on their own. By confronting the feeling and staying with it, the feeling is no longer something to be afraid of but something to take care of and nurture.

Section 4: Quick Tips for Depressed and Traumatized Adolescents

24. Turning Fear into Courage

Ages: 13-18

Purpose: To confront fears and worries and step into your full life.

Materials:

- This worksheet
- Pen/pencil

Instructions: Complete the following with the teen.

1. Having the thought "I couldn't do that, or that's too hard," happens to all of us. But sometimes these thoughts keep us from doing/being all we are meant to. Just for a moment, let's think about the other times when you did something truly amazing and courageous. Write these down here.

_____

_____

_____

2. If you are having a hard time coming up with your own courageous acts, think of a few people that you admire for their acts of bravery (big or small). Write down their names and acts of courage here.

_____

_____

_____

3. If you were one of those people, what would you have done in that situation?

_____

_____

_____

Challenging Children & Adolescents

4. For a moment, think of something that you would love to do but can't even imagine yourself doing it. Even if you can't do it, close your eyes and imagine the way it would feel to be able to. Describe it here. (Example: Flying through the air on a trapeze.)

_____
_____
_____

5. What is something that you have been afraid to say or do because you thought you wouldn't get it right or that you would fail?

_____
_____
_____

6. What or who might stand in the way of doing or saying that thing?

_____
_____
_____

7. Who do you know that would support you in accomplishing this?

_____
_____
_____

8. What are some steps that you could take right now to prepare yourself to do or say that thing?

_____
_____
_____

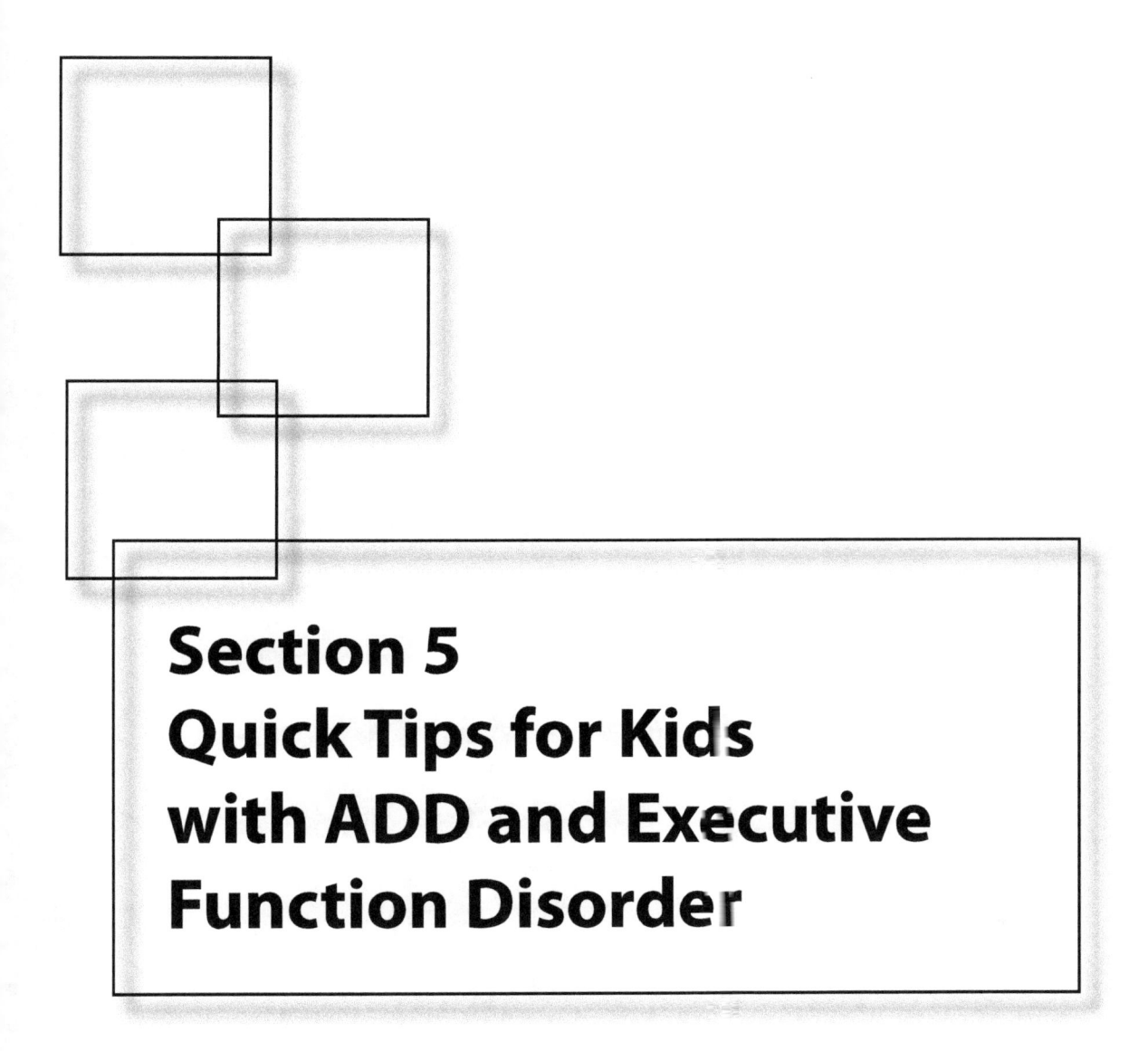

Section 5
Quick Tips for Kids with ADD and Executive Function Disorder

Checklist: Executive Function Disorder

Executive function is the name for a group of essential mental tasks, including planning, strategizing, organizing, setting goals, and paying attention to the important details that will help to achieve those goals. Executive function is what gets us down to business even when we'd rather just hang out.

What do you notice about this child or teen?

___Difficulty planning

___Problems organizing

___Problems strategizing

___Issues with goal setting

___Inattentive to details

___No self-discipline

___Can't self-regulate

___No clear sense of time

___Inability to hold many things in one's mind at once

___Problems with cooperation and teamwork

___Not open to new ideas

___Inability and unwillingness to make corrections

___Difficulty with memorization and recall

___Difficulty with questioning and researching

Section 5: Quick Tips for Kids with ADD and Executive Function Disorder

25. Any Day Tool Kit

When I was a child we had a rule that the TV did not go on during the day. We had to create our own fun and we usually had no problem thinking of something to do. What has changed in the past thirty years is that most kids don't know how to amuse themselves unless they are plugged in. That is why I came up with the "Any Day Tool Kit."

Ages: 3-9

Purpose: To encourage creativity and play, and increase self-esteem, learning and exploration. Use as a boredom buster.

Sample Activities:

1. Create with play dough. Get out the cookie cutters and let the kids make a mess. Once it dries, it is a breeze to clean up.

2. Shoe boxes, magazines, and glue sticks make great art projects. Let kids decorate the boxes and use them for storing their treasures, dreams and even worries.

3. Go through photographs, let the kids cut them up and make a collage of a family event.

4. Set up a school room and let the kids be the teachers to one another.

5. Have an indoor scavenger hunt.

6. Have a picnic lunch on beach towels and bathing suits in the family room.

7. Let the kids build a fort out of chairs and blankets.

8. Read your kids a book.

9. Give your kids a bag of objects and have them put on a play for you using the objects.

10. Sit back and watch your kids have fun, while knowing you are sparking their creative minds while feeling proud of your wonderful parenting powers!

Section 5: Quick Tips for Kids with ADD and Executive Function Disorder

26. Pom-Poms and You

Ages: 3-9

Purpose: To increase cooperation and attention. Break down overwhelming tasks into bite-size pieces and then reward the child for their effort and completion of the tasks.

Materials:

- 2 Jars (at least one clear)
- Colored pom-poms (from craft store)
- Paper cut into strips
- Markers

Instructions:

Have child complete tasks to earn pom-poms to use for a future reward/project. As the jar fills, say, "Look how many pom-poms you have earned!"

For children ages 3-5, watching the pom-poms accumulate in the jar might be enough of an incentive. After the jar is filled the pom-poms they can be used in an art activity such as gluing to paper to make a picture.

For children ages 6-9, you can give a second reward once the jar is filled. These extra rewards/motivators should not cost money; rather, they should focus on time with you the parent, teacher or therapist by doing some activity together.

Along with the child, brainstorm the activities the child would like to do with you. Here are a few ideas:

- Backwards dinner (dessert first)
- Bike ride
- Picnic lunch on the floor while watching a video
- Baking brownies or cookies
- Card/board game
- Manicure and pedicure spa night at home

Challenging Children & Adolescents

Use the markers to write the rewards on slips of paper and put them in the jar. Once the pom-poms have filled up the clear jar the child can pick a 'time-together' activity from the other jar.

Have more than one child? They can a share a jar and fill it up together encouraging teamwork and cooperation.

Example tasks to earn pom-poms:

Before school:
- Put on shirt, socks, pants, shoes
- Brush teeth/hair
- Eat breakfast and clear plate
- Ready for school with backpack at the front door

After school:
- Hang up backpack
- Each homework task
- Take bath, put on PJs, brush teeth, etc.

Focus on the problem areas or the areas where the child has not become independent.

Section 5: Quick Tips for Kids with ADD and Executive Function Disorder

27. Poker Chips for Electronics

Kids with ADD (Attention Deficit Disorder) and EFD (Executive Function Disorder) can benefit when tasks are broken down into bite-size pieces.

Ages: 9-14

Purpose: To help break down overwhelming tasks, chores, homework, and self-care. To help reduce parent-child conflict and teach kids that work comes before play.

Materials:

- Poker chips (various colors)
- Jar
- Timer

Instructions:

Decide the value of each color poker chip. (For example: Blue = 5 minutes, Red = 10 minutes, White = Bonus (you decide))

Focus on completing a task, such as getting ready for school, within a certain amount of time and mark off completed items on a check list.

- ✔ Getting dressed: Blue (5 minutes)
- ✔ Eating breakfast: Blue (5 minutes)
- ✔ Packing backpack: Blue (5 minutes)
- ✔ Making lunch: Blue (5 minutes)
- ✔ On time at the bus stop: Red (10 minutes)

This child earned a total of 30 minutes of electronics that he can use after school **BEFORE** beginning his homework.

The child turns in his chips in exchange for the time the same day or he can save all his time for another day. The timer is started at the beginning of the time according to the amount of chips exchanged. Once the chips are used, there is no more electronics until more chips are earned. Bonus chips can be used when giving extra praise for going above and beyond expectations.

Section 5: Quick Tips for Kids with ADD and Executive Function Disorder

28. Whistle While You Work: Taking Care of Our Belongings

Go to your child's room. Stand right in the middle of it. Look around. How do you feel? If you say exhausted, overwhelmed or frustrated…good! That is exactly how your child feels when sent there to clean it up.

Ages: 5-18

Purpose: To teach children/teens how to break down overwhelming projects into bite-size pieces and promote having fun with chores and reduce parent/child conflict.

Materials:

- 3×5 cards
- Markers

Instructions: On each card, write a step that is involved in cleaning up the bedroom.

>   Some examples are:
>   *Laundry from floor into hamper*
>   *Toys back in bins*
>   *Dishes, glasses to dishwasher*
>   *Books on shelves*
>   *Games picked up and stored in boxes*
>   *Clean clothes hung up/put away*

When your child comes home from school tell her that you are going to help her clean up her room. Hand her one of the cards and tell her to do what is on the card and then come back to you with the card completed. Put a sticker on the back of the card or draw a happy face to show it was completed. Hand her the next card and so on. Do this every day until your child starts automatically putting things where they belong.

Hints:
>   *If your child cannot read, draw pictures on each card representing the item to be picked up.
>   *For teens, use cards or a checklist. Ask them which they would like to use.
>   *Keep the cards in a basket in an easily accessible place.
>   *Add a timer for more fun!

Section 5: Quick Tips for Kids with ADD and Executive Function Disorder

29. Give Them a Hook

Ages: 3-18

Purpose: To provide an environment where children can learn and practice organizational skills and to reduce parent-child conflict. Helps assist children with ADD and EFD.

Instructions:

- **Family calendar.** Track everyone's activities on a large calendar that is hung where everyone can see it (kitchen, for example). Assign each family member their own color marker for their entries. Always reference the calendar when making plans. Bring the calendar to your weekly family meeting.

- **Checklists.** Create lists on 3 x 5 cards for all activities that have multiple steps, such as bed time (shower, brush teeth, read story). Encourage your child to create the cards with you.

- **Focus on chores that involve sorting or categorizing.** Grocery shopping, folding laundry (matching socks), emptying the dishwasher and putting dishes away, and other tasks that involve pre-planning, making lists, or arranging things are great choices.

- **Always get ready the night before.** Pack lunches, backpacks and lay out clothing to make the morning a breeze and teach your child the importance of planning in advance.

- **Use containers and closet organizers.** Everything has its place. Take photos of toys, clothing and personal items and tape them to the outside of the container where you want them stored (think kindergarten classroom).

- **Cook together.** Cooking teaches measuring, following directions, sorting ingredients, and managing time — all key elements in organization. Even cleaning up and putting utensils and pans back where they belong makes the task that much easier for the next time.

- **Collecting.** If your child has a particular interest, encourage him or her to create and organize a collection. Use creativity in this area and you don't have to spend a penny (think the great outdoors).

- **Be a role model.** Remember that if you are disorganized your child will follow your lead. Always put things back where they live, keep your living space clear of clutter and hang up your coat!

Section 5: Quick Tips for Kids with ADD and Executive Function Disorder

30. Behavior Charts that Really Work

Ages: 3-9

Purpose: To encourage "start" behaviors—what you want children to do more often. A new twist to the old chart!

Instructions: Encourage parents to fill out this worksheet to create a behavior chart that really works!

1. If you could wave a magic wand over your child's negative behavior, what behaviors would go away because of the impact they have on you and your family?

    1. _____
    2. _____
    3. _____
    4. _____
    5. _____
    6. _____
    7. _____
    8. _____
    9. _____
    10. _____

2. Now looking over your list, select three behaviors that are creating the most negative impact on you and the rest of the family.

    1. _____
    2. _____
    3. _____

Challenging Children & Adolescents

3. Now prioritize them. Rate these from 1 to 3 in importance of getting the biggest bang for your buck:

   1. _____

   2. _____

   3. _____

4. Let's say that you have chosen "Joey" kicking and hitting his little brother as the number 1 priority. What would you like to see from Joey instead? "Be kinder to his brother, play nicely, and keep his hands and feet to himself." Right! What we did was to take the negative and turn it around to a positive. Write down the new positive behavior here:

   _____

*Remember to focus on the positive: "I want to see my child playing nicely. Rather than saying, I want my child to stop kicking and hitting his brother."

Every time you notice Joey playing nicely with another child, go to the chart and draw a happy face on it. The younger the child, the more frequent the tracking/praise needs to be. The key is to focus on only one behavior at a time. When this behavior improves you can move on to priority #2, and so forth.

Joey plays nicely with another child

☺	☺				

For very young children, getting the happy face will be enough. With an older child you can tell them that if they earn X amount of happy faces they can pick from the reward jar. Just like the pom-poms (see Pom-Poms and You #26), the best reward is time with you!

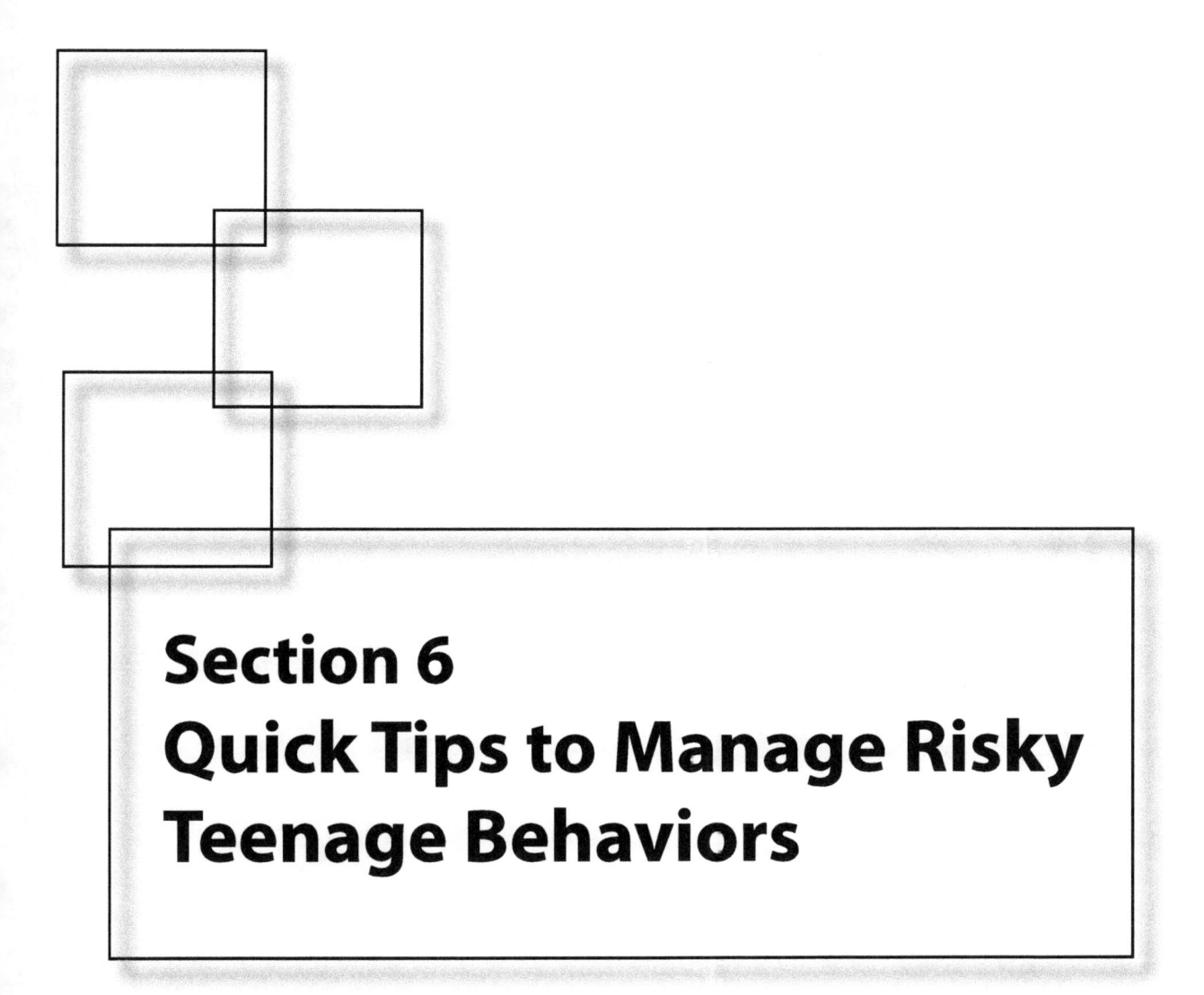

Section 6
Quick Tips to Manage Risky Teenage Behaviors

Section 6: Quick Tips to Manage Risky Teenage Behaviors

31. Difficult Conversations: Parent Guide

Sex, drugs, STDs, HIV, and AIDS are all subjects that most parents have difficulty bringing up with their kids. Think back to when you were a child. Who told you about sex? Was it a friend? Was it your mom or dad? If so, how did they handle it and what information did you receive? Was this information accurate? Or did you learn about it on your own as you were experiencing your first relationship? What was your religious upbringing? Were you told that sex was dirty or natural? Were you told to wait until marriage? Or did your mom bring you to the doctor to have you put on birth control? Did your dad hand you condoms and pat you on the back? Our own teenage experiences often have a huge impact on our parenting. We may agree or disagree with our parents on how these subjects were presented or ignored. So before you venture into these difficult conversations with your child or teen look back at how they were handled in your life.

Ages: As soon as possible

Purpose: To foster open communication between parents and children/adolescents. To provide guidance and education about the risks associated with choices.

Instructions:

Therapist: Share the following script with parents and rehearse/role-play so that they can have these difficult conversations at home.

> **1. Get clear about your own morals and values.** (Supplemental worksheet follows)
>
> How do you feel about teens having sex? Do you have different rules for your own teen?
>
> What do you think about kids smoking marijuana?
>
> What do you think about underage drinking? 18, 19, 20 year olds? When is it okay? When is it not?

Challenging Children & Adolescents

2. Educate yourself about the issues you want to discuss with your kids.

Get on the internet and bring up articles about current trends for youth. Make sure that you have the most up-to-date information about the areas that you are focusing on. Remember, not only are you providing parental guidance but you are also passing along knowledge that your child will need to make thoughtful and appropriate decisions about his or her emotional and physical health.

Learn/use their language. (Kids don't call marijuana "pot" anymore.) Do you know what the following are? If not, look them up!

DXM, syrup heads, dexing, triple, special k, crank, antifreeze, crunk, snow, X, Georgia Home Boy, roofies, kibbles and bits, cheese, candy flipping

3. Make Time to Talk to Your Child

Once you know what you want to talk about and have done your research, it is time. If you are nervous or anxious about having this conversation, acknowledge this to your child. "This is really hard and uncomfortable for me to speak with you about, but I am your parent and I need to talk with you about…" Be prepared that your child may react negatively to you or say that they "already know all that…" Proceed anyway. Give your child printed information or websites to back up what you are saying. If your child argues with you, tell him/her that you would be glad to hear what s/he has to say, but first s/he must research the topic and present it to you just like you did.

Don't wait too long to have these conversations. Kids are experimenting with sex and drugs earlier and earlier. The younger you start, the easier it will be to continue bringing it up. A great conversation starter might be after you and your child have seen a movie with sex or drugs within the content. "What did you think about that movie? What did you think about the choices that (fill in character name) made? What would you have done? Do you have any questions about anything that you saw?"

If your child ignores you or doesn't want to talk about it, don't give up! Keep looking for opportunities to bring up those uncomfortable issues. Soon you will notice that it isn't so awkward after all!

Parent Worksheet: Difficult Conversations

How do you feel about teens having sex?

_____
_____

Do you have different rules for your own teen?

_____
_____

What do you think about kids smoking marijuana?

_____
_____

What do you think about underage drinking? 18, 19, 20 year olds? When is it okay? When is it not?

_____
_____

What are the drugs of choice in your community?

_____
_____

How much supervision do teens really need?

_____
_____

*Opportunities for discussions: movies at home, TV shows, car rides

Sample Parent and Teen Contract: Out with Friends Unsupervised

I know that going out with my friends without parental supervision is a privilege. I respect that you love me and want to keep me safe. You respect that I am no longer a small child and want the privilege of going out with my friends without your supervision. Therefore, we both agree:

1. I will always tell you where I am going to be, who I am going to be with, and what I am going to be doing.

2. If I am going to be at a friend's house, I will share the address and phone number with you.

3. My curfew is _____. This can be negotiated between us. My curfew means that I am inside my home.

4. I understand that I must let you know as soon as I come home.

5. I will always call and ask your permission if my plans have changed and will not go anywhere without checking in with you first.

6. I understand that you have the right and responsibility to check up on me not only when you feel the need, but from time to time just to keep me safe.

7. I will respect the limits and guidelines of my friend's parents.

8. I agree that if I am unable to keep up with my responsibilities, such as my school work and chores, I can lose the privilege of going out with my friends.

9. I understand that I can call you at any time if I feel threatened or unsafe when I am out with my friends. I will not have consequences for getting myself out of a bad situation.

10. The consequences for not following through with these guidelines for going out with friends unsupervised are:

    1. _____
    2. _____
    3. _____

Teen Signature_____   Date_____

Parent Signature_____   Date_____

Section 6: Quick Tips to Manage Risky Teenage Behaviors

32. Parents as Good Role Models for Teen Drivers

Before you drive anywhere in your car this morning, think about some of the messages you are sending to your kids and start acting like you want your kids to act.

- Wear seatbelts.
- Don't exhibit road rage.
- Don't use the cell phone.
- Avoid distraction.
- Don't tailgate.
- Don't drink and drive...ever.
- Be courteous to other drivers.
- Take care of your car inside and out.

Write up a contract with your teen that explicitly states the rules and responsibilities of driving (sample contract follows).

Issues to address are:

- Consequences for drinking/using drugs while driving
- Speeding and cell phone use
- Curfew with the car
- Who pays for what (gas, insurance, upkeep, etc.)
- Insist that driving and use of the car is a privilege and not a rite of passage into adulthood.

Parents and teens will sign the contract and then post it in a prominent area of the house so there are no arguments, no exceptions. Break the rules, lose the privilege.

Sample Parent and Teen Contract: Teen Driving

I know that being able to drive the family car is a privilege. I respect that you love me and want to keep me safe. You respect that I am growing up and want the privilege of using the family car. Therefore, we agree:

1. I will follow the rules of the road, staying within speed limits.

2. I only have permission to use the car at these times: _____.

3. I must be home with the car by: _____.

4. I agree not to use my cell phone, MP3 player or other electronic device while driving.

5. I agree to not leave the gas tank empty at any time and to contribute my share to gas. My share is: _____.

6. I agree to pay my share of the car insurance. My share is:_____.

7. I agree to follow the law and your rules about having other people in the car. These laws and rules are as follows:_____

8. I agree to always wear my seatbelt.

9. I agree to call you if I am unable to drive the car for any reason.

10. I will not use alcohol, marijuana or any other drug while operating the car and will not transport anyone who is using.

   The consequences for not following through with these limits are:

   1._____

   2._____

   3._____

Teen Signature _____   Date _____

Parent Signature_____   Date_____

Section 6: Quick Tips to Manage Risky Teenage Behaviors

33. Parents: What You Need to Know About Your Teen and Drugs and Alcohol

Do you suspect that your teen is using or abusing alcohol or drugs? Is there a nagging feeling in the back of your mind that tells you that you really need to check this out? Are you afraid of what you might find? Do you worry when your son or daughter is out with friends for hours on end and you don't know where they really are?

Then join the ranks of parents raising teens today in America. In almost every interaction I have with parents of teenagers the topic of drugs & alcohol comes up. Parents don't know what to do.

Should I search his room? Should I confront her? Should I demand a drug test? Will I drive an even bigger wedge into our already distant relationship? Maybe it's just normal that she is experimenting…but her moods have changed. I am frightened for my teen's safety.

Then read on:

Warning signs of teen alcohol or drug abuse:

- Missing school or work
- Not saying where s/he is going; or being vague about where s/he has been
- Lying about where s/he has been
- Stopping activities that s/he used to enjoy and not replacing them with other fun activities
- Borrowing money from parents or friends and unable to explain loss of money or valuables
- Sniffling, runny nose, dilated pupils or red eyes
- Loss of appetite or eating too much
- Associating with a new group of friends, maybe those who use drugs
- Hiding things that would show alcohol or drug use: liquor bottles, rolling papers or pipes
- Moodiness, change in personality, avoiding you

(Source: National Institute on Drug Abuse)

Challenging Children & Adolescents

What you can do:

Parental Monitoring: Supervise your teen or know where your teen is and what they are doing.

Make a Plan: Decide what you will say before you talk to your teen if you suspect alcohol or drug abuse. (Avoid negativity and express your concerns with care and love.)

State the Facts: State what you know from the above warning signs.

Be Open: Listen to what your teen has to say.

Set and Enforce Rules: With care and concern, let your teen know that you will not put up with drug or alcohol use/abuse. "I know you can't stand it when I make rules, but I am your parent and it is my job to keep you safe." Hold your teen accountable for his or her actions and set clear consequences for not obeying your rules.

Be Prepared for Obstacles: Many teens will become very angry and defensive and walk away from you. Take a deep breath and go back for round #2.

Keep Talking: Any chance you get, make an attempt to talk with your teen. Don't give up or lose your temper no matter how uncomfortable the situation might seem.

Design a Contract: The contract should outline the rules and their consequences; both you and your teen need to sign it. Be clear, firm and concise.

Follow Through: Be consistent. The minute you back off or avoid your teen, they will run with the freedom.

Know This: Your teen wants you to rein him or her in. It is scary having so much power and no one noticing that you are getting away with breaking rules. Being out of control is not that much fun for your teen either.

Section 6: Quick Tips to Manage Risky Teenage Behaviors

34. Parent Ammo: The Written Word

Getting through to a teen that is in denial can be impossible. One method that has good results is research and the printed word. The following parent did research and then confronted the teen with the physical complaints that he was using not to go to school. The teen was denying using marijuana.

Dear Susan {therapist},

Here is an excerpt from an article on the effects of long term marijuana use. It really took away Joey's excuses especially after all the medical tests showed he was in otherwise good health.

I highlighted below the symptoms that Joey has and deleted some parts of the article which were long winded so that Joey would at least look at it. He smiled and I think he said I "booked him" which means he's not getting away with it anymore.

Keeping fingers crossed.

> **Short-term effects of using marijuana include**
> - **Sleepiness**
> - Difficulty keeping track of time
> - Reduced ability to perform tasks requiring concentration and coordination, such as driving a car
> - **Increased heart rate**
> - Potential cardiac dangers for those with preexisting heart disease
> - Bloodshot eyes
> - **Dry mouth and throat**
> - Decreased social inhibitions
> - Paranoia, hallucinations
> - Impaired or reduced short-term memory
> - Impaired or reduced comprehension
> - Altered motivation and cognition, making the acquisition of new information difficult
> - Psychological dependence
> - Impairments in learning, memory, perception, and judgment - difficulty speaking, listening effectively, thinking, retaining knowledge, problem solving, and forming concepts
> - **Intense anxiety** or panic attacks

Challenging Children & Adolescents

Long-term effects of using marijuana include:
- Enhanced cancer risk
- Decrease in testosterone levels and lower sperm counts for men
- Increase in testosterone levels for women and increased risk of infertility
- Diminished or extinguished sexual pleasure
- Psychological dependence requiring more of the drug to get the same effect

What is THC?

THC is the chemical in marijuana which makes you feel "high" (which means experiencing a change in mood and seeing or feeling things differently). Certain parts of the plant contain higher levels of THC. The flowers or buds have more THC than the stems or leaves.

The Effect of THC

When marijuana is smoked, THC goes:
- quickly into the blood through the lungs
- to the brain (this is when the "high" is felt and can happen within a few minutes and can last up to five hours)

THC is absorbed more slowly into the blood when marijuana is eaten as it has to pass through the stomach and intestine and can take up to one hour to experience the "high" effects which can last up to 12 hours.

THC is absorbed quickly into body fat and is then released very slowly back into the blood. This process can take up to one month for a single dose of THC to fully leave the body.

Effects

The effects of marijuana will vary from person to person depending on:
- Amount taken
- How strong (potent) the marijuana is
- How the marijuana is taken (joint, bong, food)
- Size, weight, health
- Mood
- Individual experience with marijuana
- If marijuana is taken with other drugs
- Whether alone or with other people, at home or at a party

Section 6: Quick Tips to Manage Risky Teenage Behaviors

Because marijuana users often inhale the unfiltered smoke deeply and then hold it in their lungs as long as possible, marijuana is damaging to the lungs and pulmonary system. Marijuana smoke contains some of the same carcinogens and toxic particulates as tobacco, sometimes in higher concentrations. Long-term users of cannabis may develop psychological dependence and require more of the drug to get the same effect. The drug can become the center of their lives.

The Effects on the Male:

Marijuana is the most common drug used by adolescents in America today. Marijuana affects the parts of the brain which control the sex and growth hormones. In males, marijuana can decrease the testosterone level. Occasional cases of enlarged breasts in male marijuana users can be triggered by the chemical impact on the hormone system. Regular marijuana use can also lead to a decrease in sperm count, as well as increases in abnormal and immature sperm. Marijuana is a contributing factor in the rising problem of infertility in males. Young males should know the potential effects of marijuana use on sex and the growing process before they decide to smoke marijuana.

Effects of Marijuana on the Brain:

Researchers have found that THC changes the way in which sensory information gets into and is acted on by the hippocampus. This is a component of the brain's limbic system that is crucial for learning, memory, and the integration of sensory experiences with emotions and motivations. Investigations have shown that neurons in the information processing system of the hippocampus and the activity of the nerve fibers are suppressed by THC. In addition, researchers have discovered that learned behaviors, which depend on the hippocampus, also deteriorate. Recent research findings also indicate that long-term use of marijuana produces changes in the brain similar to those seen after long-term use of other major drugs of abuse.

Effects on the Lungs:

Someone who smokes marijuana regularly may have many of the same respiratory problems that tobacco smokers have. These individuals may have a **daily cough and phlegm, symptoms of chronic bronchitis, and more frequent chest colds.** Continuing to smoke marijuana can lead to abnormal functioning of lung tissue injured or destroyed by marijuana smoke.

Regardless of the THC content, the amount of tar and the level of carbon monoxide inhaled and absorbed by marijuana smokers are three to five times greater than among tobacco smokers. This may be due to the marijuana users inhaling more deeply and holding the smoke in the lungs.

Challenging Children & Adolescents

Effects on Heart Rate and Blood Pressure:

Recent findings indicate that smoking marijuana while shooting up cocaine has the potential to cause severe increases in heart rate and blood pressure. In one study, experienced marijuana and cocaine users were given marijuana alone, cocaine alone, and then a combination of both. Each drug alone produced cardiovascular effects. When they were combined, the effects were greater and lasted longer. The heart rate of the subjects in the study increased by 29 beats per minute with marijuana alone and by 32 beats per minute with cocaine alone. When the drugs were given together, the heart rate increased by 49 beats per minute, and the increased rate persisted for a longer time. The drugs were given with the subjects sitting quietly. In other circumstances, an individual may smoke marijuana and inject cocaine and then do something physically stressful which may significantly increase risks of overload on the cardiovascular system.

Effects of Heavy Marijuana Use on Learning and Social Behavior:

A study of college students has shown that critical skills related to attention, memory, and learning are impaired among people who use marijuana heavily, even after discontinuing its use for at least 24 hours. Researchers compared 65 "heavy users," who had smoked marijuana a median of 29 of the past 30 days, and 64 "light users," who had smoked a median of 1 of the past 30 days. After a closely monitored 19- to 24-hour period of abstinence from marijuana and other illicit drugs and alcohol, the users were given several standard tests measuring aspects of attention, memory, and learning. Compared to the light users, heavy marijuana users made more errors and had more difficulty sustaining attention, shifting attention to meet the demands of changes in the environment, and in registering, processing, and using information. The findings suggest that the greater impairment among heavy users is likely due to an alteration of brain activity produced by marijuana.

Longitudinal research on marijuana use among young people below college age indicates those who use have lower achievement than the non-users, more acceptance of deviant behavior, more delinquent behavior and aggression, greater rebelliousness, poorer relationships with parents, and more associations with delinquent and drug-using friends.

Write Me an Essay

Ages: 13-18

Purpose: To educate teens about the consequences of their choices.

Instructions:

- Assign an essay according to the situation
- Guidelines for the teen:
    - Length: 250-500 words, double-spaced, spellchecked
    - Must be at least a "B" paper
    - No privileges until paper is turned in to the parent and discussed together

Topic examples:

- Marijuana's Effect on a Teenage Boy's Brain

- How AIDS/HIV is Contracted and What Happens to Your Body

- What is Date Rape and What You Can Do to be Safe

- Drinking and Driving: Why It is Dangerous

- Texting and Driving: Why It is Dangerous

- Available Jobs and Pay for Kids Who Don't Finish High School

- Prescription Drugs and Addictions

Section 7
Quick Tips on How to Command Respect Minus the Fear Factor

Section 7: Quick Tips on How to Command Respect Minus the Fear Factor

35. Which Behaviors Do You Want to Stop?

Behaviors that annoy, disrupt, disturb and are hurtful can show up in kids in many different ways. These can be irritating and they can also be quite severe and interfere with functioning, relationships and academics. Let's first identify these behaviors by listing them out. (Not listening is not a "stop" behavior…whereas "ignoring" is.)

List what you want the child/teen to stop doing: (For example: talking back, gesturing or other disruptive behaviors)

1.

2.

3.

4.

5.

Section 7: Quick Tips on How to Command Respect Minus the Fear Factor

36. Commanding Respect

You love your child. You want them to be as great as you know they can be. You want them to grow up healthy with their head on straight. But, somewhere along the line they got "derailed" and started on a path that's led to tremendous stress and anxiety for everyone. Pick your poison. Is your child:

- Angry?
- Defiant?
- Disrespectful?
- Unmotivated?

The harder you try to control the situation, the more out of control things get. Maybe they get better for a very brief time (and you hope it will stay this way), but it never lasts and the next big blow up is always just around the corner.

Case Example

Joey screams at and talks back to his parents all the time. He is constantly picking fights with his younger brothers. He is so angry that his mother, "Sharon," is afraid that he is scaring the other children and she hates to admit it but she is often afraid of him, too. How horrible, to be afraid of her own son! Mom and dad have gone around and around trying to fix this. They have talked to numerous professionals, tried therapy, and even medications for their son.

Here is Their Story

Last year, Sharon took Joey to a therapist, more like she dragged him to the appointments. The therapist told her that he doesn't talk and there is not much he can do with him if Joey won't talk in the sessions. The therapist told Sharon to take Joey to an MD because maybe he is depressed or bi-polar.

SO, Sharon followed the therapist's advice, took Joey to an MD, and the MD prescribed 3 different medications. Sharon had to fight with Joey every day to take the medications and if that wasn't bad enough, Joey seemed worse. Instead of acting angry he wouldn't come out of his room. She cancelled the next appointment with the MD and stopped giving Joey the medications. Within 2 weeks Joey started up with the loud angry outbursts. Living this way was taking a toll on the entire family. Sharon is even noticing that her and her husband are fighting more and no one in the family is talking to each other. It is like everyone is hiding out!

Challenging Children & Adolescents

Angry kids are not going to cooperate; therefore, YOU must put a stop to back talk, interrupting, face making and other negative body language. Well, you say, "Easier said than done!" Actually, it is simple. The glitch is that it takes consistency and a poker face from you. Every time your child engages in one of these negative behaviors, you have to block him/her.

You ask, "**EVERY TIME? ARE YOU CRAZY?** How do I do that?"

Here's the drill:
You say to your son or daughter: "Do not speak to me that way."
Or "Do not interrupt me."
Or "Do not make that face."
AND the catch, you have to keep saying it until s/he stops and you must remain calm and not give up until s/he stops the behavior.

Do not let this behavior slide. You need to be **ON** 100% of the time. So pick a day that you are rested and in fairly good spirits, have someone you can call for support if you feel yourself caving.

Setting Up Expectations

Good. Now you have his/her attention and respect. Let's talk about setting up expectations.

- You do not want your son/daughter hurting or threatening your other children.

- Spell it out. Tell him/her directly that this is unacceptable behavior.

- Then tell him/her what the consequence will be if this happens.

The glitch? You have to follow through with the consequence.

A word about consequences: Don't overdo them. Grounding your child for a month will be more of a hardship for you than for your kid. Remember, you will have to see that face day in and day out, begging you to reconsider.

Think of a consequence that is swift and logical. I personally like community service. An example of this: Do something nice for or with the person that you hurt. (Maybe take over one of their chores or help them with their homework.)

Section 7: Quick Tips on How to Command Respect Minus the Fear Factor

37. Watch Out for Negativity

How do you speak to your child? Do you feel angry and resentful about their behavior? Do you feel that all you focus on is the negative?

Then stay with me…
Let's try something new.

Here we go:

80% of the time you will focus on your child's strengths—that only leaves 20% negativity. How does that sound?

It is all in the way you phrase it.

- "Is something not going the way it is supposed to?"
- "I know you are trying really hard to control your temper and I see you catching yourself when you begin to lose it. Is there anything I can do to help you?"

You are validating that he is trying while also offering support and help. This will give him motivation and incentive to try even harder. You can also take the blame off him and put it on the situation. This helps to prevent defensiveness.

A word about OVERPROTECTION (this does not mean "not letting him do the things he wants"): Overprotection means that you make excuses for his behavior even though he is out of control. Another word for this is enabling. If you blame others or the school, does not mean you are being positive toward your child. It means that you are letting him off the hook.

Remember, decreasing negativity towards your child has a direct effect on eliciting more positive behaviors!

Section 7: Quick Tips on How to Command Respect Minus the Fear Factor

38. Provide Nurturance and Guidance

Teach your child empathy for others. Let him/her know that his/her actions affect you and others.

Example: Parent observes 9-year-old poking his 5-year-old brother.

Typical parent response: "Leave your brother alone! Go to your room!!"

Teaching empathy and relationship building response:

> **Dad:** "Joey, is what you are doing making your brother happy?"
> **Joey:** "No."
> **Dad:** "Why would you do something to make your brother unhappy?"
> **Joey:** "I'm bored."
> **Dad:** "Joey, do you enjoy planning with Jason?"
> **Joey:** "Yes."
> **Dad:** "Jason, do you enjoy playing with Joey?"
> **Jason:** "Yes."
> **Dad:** "How about we find something you two can play together that you both enjoy?"

Demonstrate the skill of problem solving by showing your child how to process a situation and get to a resolution.

- **Hold your child accountable for the expectations and the rules that you have created.**
  "How will I know that you have completed the chores that I asked you to do?"

- **Share stories of your childhood.**
  Kids love to hear about when you were younger and what you learned from your own experiences.

- **Connect with your child.**
  Make eye contact at least 10 times daily with your child. Ask open ended questions—avoid yes or no questions.

Providing nurturance and guidance creates loving, giving and kind children.

Section 7: Quick Tips on How to Command Respect Minus the Fear Factor

39. Listen for Feelings

Look past the content of what your child is expressing.

- What feelings are you noticing? Anger, sadness, disappointment, resentment, jealousy, frustration, happiness, joy?

- Check in with your child about his/her feelings.

- Comment on what you see and ask your child if you are reading him/her correctly.

- Validate his/her feelings.
    "I know you are frustrated that your curfew is 11:00PM, do you want to talk about it?"

- Be open to negotiating if it feels right to you. You will not be spoiling your child.

- Remember, s/he has finally given up the power and maybe getting something in return will seal the deal. Everybody wins!
    "Mom, I feel different, everyone else gets to stay out until 11:30PM."

- Respond clearly and concisely.
    "Joey, I would be willing to do that but this is what I need from you:
    1. Tell me where you are going.
    2. Call me if you change locations.
    3. Do not arrive even 1 minute after 11:30PM.
    Can you do this? And remember Joey, if you are even 1 minute late you will not go out next Saturday night."

- Listening for feelings creates connection and bonding and love, love, love!!

Worksheet: Emotional Hot Buttons and Losing It! Child and Adolescent Behaviors that Drive Adults Nuts

1. Talking back

2. Swearing

3. Threatening to leave/running away/live with other parent

4. Ignoring you/walking away

5. Having to repeat yourself over and over and over

6. Inappropriate body language

7. Continual cell phone/texting

What else?

8. _____

9. _____

10. _____

Section 7: Quick Tips on How to Command Respect Minus the Fear Factor

40. Mindful Robotic Parenting

Mindfulness can be a powerful tool for changing emotional reactions and automatic thinking that undermine our parenting effectiveness. Like many other parenting techniques, Mindful Robotic Parenting is a practice which becomes stronger and more effective as we repeatedly apply it to our lives.

1. Identify two reaction patterns that you would like to begin changing. For example, becoming angry or impatient with your child.

2. List some reasons why you think you might have these habitual reaction patterns.

3. List some reason why you would like to change these reaction patterns.

4. Set a personal reminder to apply the **STOP-BREATHE-REFLECT-CHOOSE** robotic mindfulness technique to the two reaction patterns you have indentified (see next page).

5. Monitor your experiment with this practice:

    - Did you remember to use the 4-step process?

    - Was there any change in your reaction?

    - How did the experiment feel?

    - Did you notice any resources that became available to you in applying the mindfulness practice?

Parent Worksheet: 4-Step Process

Age: Parents

Materials:

- 3x5 index cards

Purpose: To encourage mindfulness in parents.

Instructions: Create 4 cue cards (as in Visual Cue Cards #10) for yourself:

STOP
BREATHE
REFLECT
CHOOSE

On the back of the **STOP** card, write:
- What am I feeling?
- Where am I feeling it in my body?
- It is okay to feel this feeling.

On the back of the **BREATHE** card, write:
- Breathe in and out slowly 5 times and notice my breath.
- Repeat: "I am okay."
- Observe the negative feeling soften.

On the back of the **REFLECT** card, write:
- How have I reacted in the past?
- How far back can I remember reacting that way?
- Who can support me here and now?
- What are my options?

On the back of the **CHOOSE** card, write:
- What are my choices/options?
- What is my best choice?
- Choose that now.

Use these cards to assist you in remaining calm and choosing how you want to respond to your child/teen.

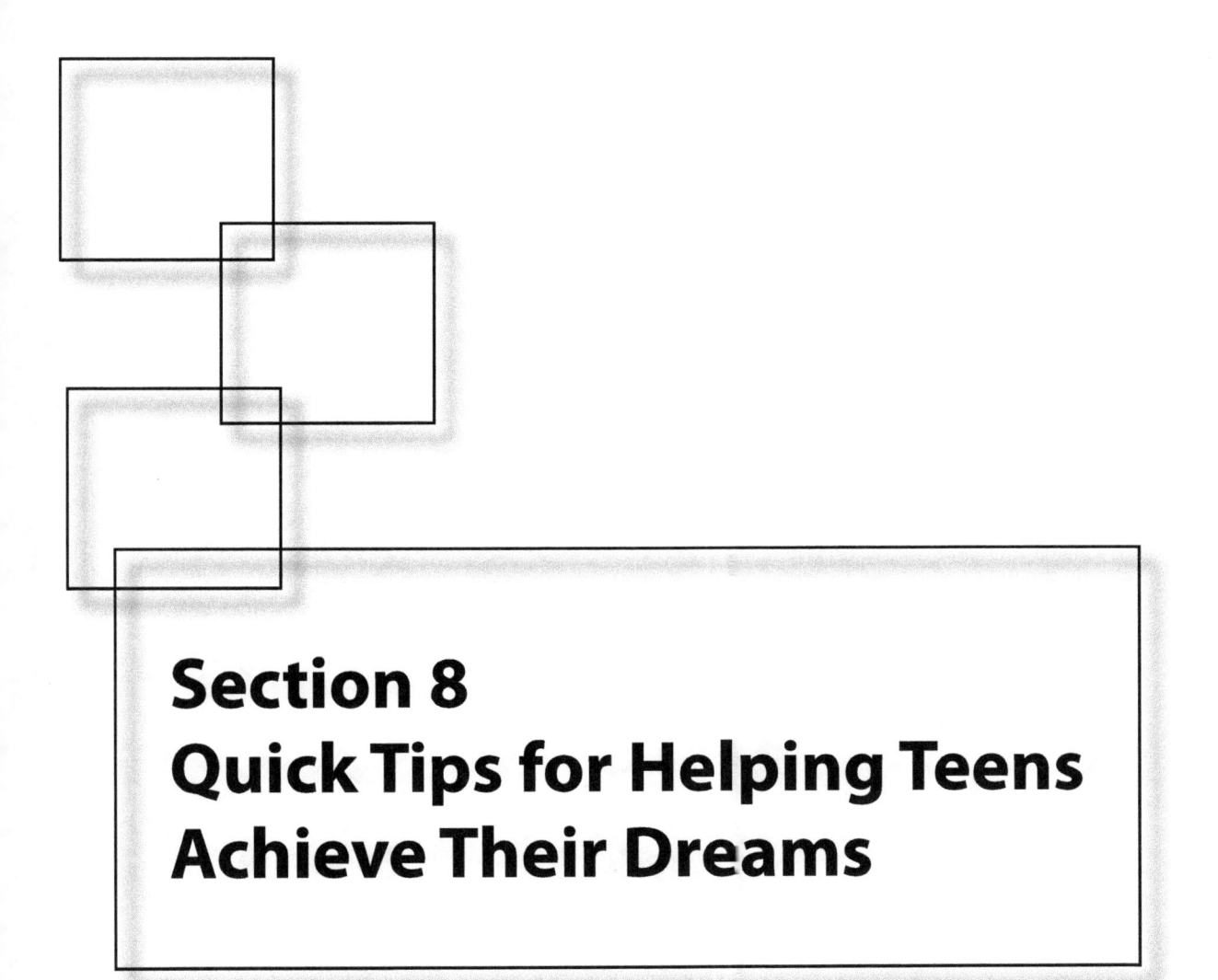

Section 8
Quick Tips for Helping Teens Achieve Their Dreams

Section 8: Quick Tips for Helping Teens Achieve Their Dreams

41. Teen's Wheel of Life: Assessment and Tracking

Ages: 13-18

Purpose: To engage teens in talking about the different segments of their lives. It can be used week to week to set goals and monitor growth.

Instructions:

- Tell child/teen to rate on a scale of 0 to 10 with 0 being "Not at All Satisfied or Happy With" to 10 being "Completely Satisfied or Happy With" that aspect of his/her life. (where the lines intersect in the middle = 0).
- Ask them to draw a line on the triangle and number it.
- Ask them to pick an area to discuss and continue to move around the wheel.

Questions to spark discussion:

- What do you make of it?
- How does this look to you?
- How do you feel about it?
- Can you say more?
- How does that fit in with your plans?
- What do you think that means?
- What do you want?

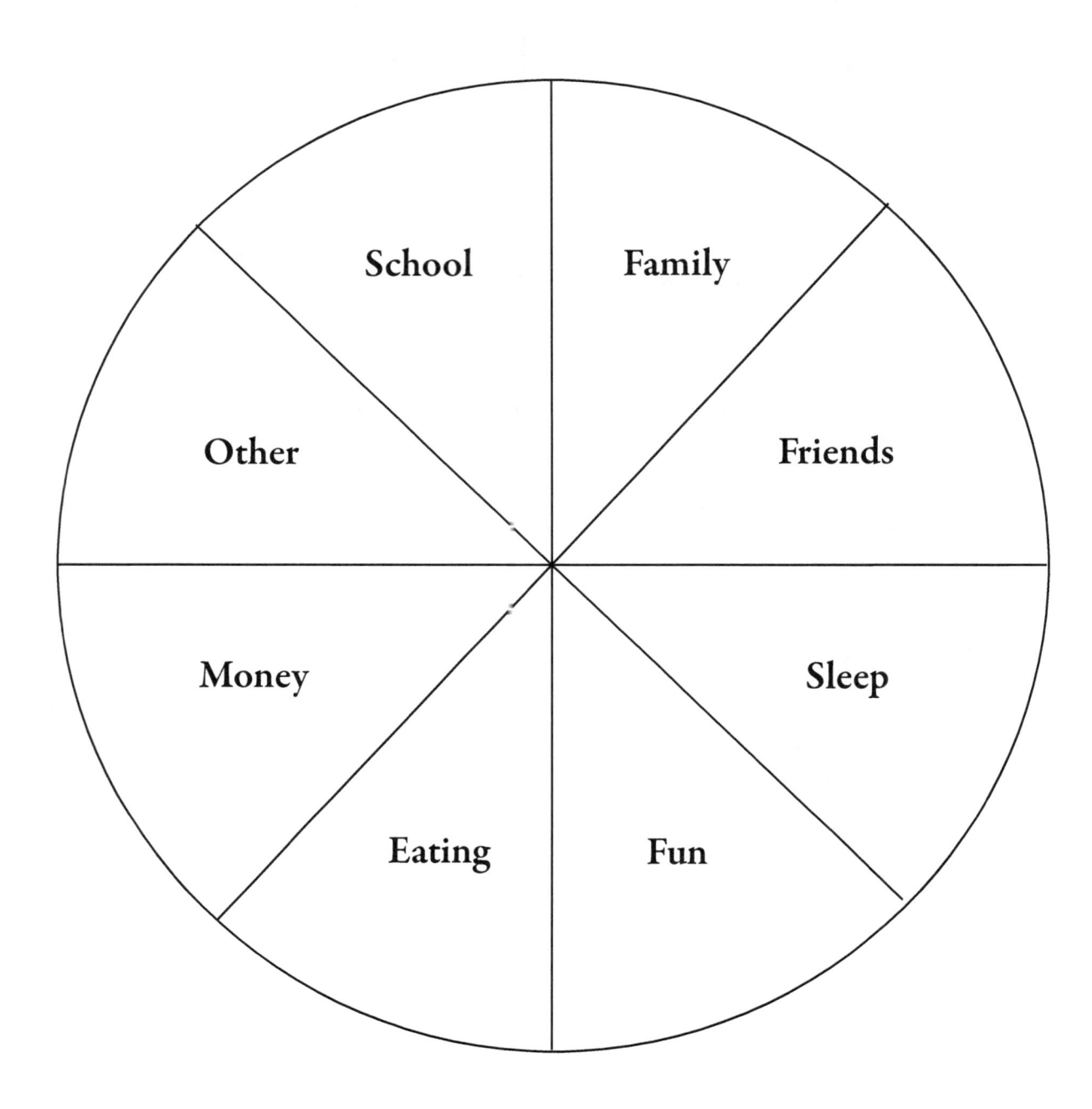

	School	Family	
Other			Friends
Money			Sleep
	Eating	Fun	

Debriefing the Wheel

Purpose: To deepen the experience and get to the core of the issues. To create a plan of action and accountability.

Instructions:

- Pick an area to tell me about.

    - If _____ was a color, what color would it be?

    - If _____ was a fabric, what would it feel like?

    - If _____ was an 8 or a 9, what would it look like?

    - What is one thing you can do this week to move up ½ point?

- Give the teen markers or colored pencils to decorate and/or shade in the different triangles on the wheel.

- Date the wheel.

- Use this exercise from time to time to demonstrate progress or to pick a new area to work on.

Section 8: Quick Tips for Helping Teens Achieve Their Dreams

42. Coach a Teen: Getting Started

Ages: 13-18

Purpose: To structure the session and create a sense of safety and control for the teen.

Instructions: Ask the teen to take a few minutes at the start of your session to answer the following questions. If s/he has a hard time coming up with anything…assist by asking the other questions below.

1. What were your successes since we last saw each other?

2. What were your challenges?

3. What would you like help with or to talk about today?

Extra Questions:

Would you like to brainstorm some ideas?

What was the best part of your week?

What was the worst part of your week?

What's happened since we last spoke?

Worksheet: Teen Coaching Check-In

Name_____   Date_____

What were your successes since we last saw each other?

1.

2.

3.

4.

5.

What were your challenges?

1.

2.

3.

4.

5.

What would you like help with or to talk about today?

1.

2.

3.

4.

5.

Section 8: Quick Tips for Helping Teens Achieve Their Dreams

43. Dear Best Friend

Ages: 13-18

Purpose: To instill motivation, hope and a sense of control over their futures through a visioning exercise for teens.

Instructions: Read this to the teen:

It's about a year from now, __ (teen) ____. You are looking back over the past year knowing that you have worked through a lot. You are no longer feeling _____ and _____; in fact, you are very satisfied with your current life. You sit down to write a letter to your best friend, describing the year. The letter starts with:

Dear __ (friend) ___,

- Next, give the teen the outline on the next page and ask them to answer the questions in a letter to their best friend.

- If needed, help the teen construct the letter to their best friend.

Worksheet: Dear Best Friend

What were your successes in the past year?

What were your challenges in the past year?

Who did you have to be to overcome those obstacles?

What did you discover/learn about yourself during the past 12 months?

Section 8: Quick Tips for Helping Teens Achieve Their Dreams

44. Visions of Hope: "If You Could Wave a Magic Wand…"

Take the teenager through this series of questions to help them get in touch with their dreams and desires.

- If you could wave a magic wand, where would you like your _____ (aspect of life) _____ (grades, motivation, relationship, goals, life, etc.) to be at within the next _____ (timeframe) _____ (six months, one year, 5 years)?

- If it turned out just like that, what would that give you?

- What would be the best part about it?

- Why?

- Back to the present, what do you think could be slowing you down or getting in the way of having what you described just now?

- Anything else?

- The way things are right now, how is this affecting your (grades, motivation, relationship, choices, life, etc.)?

- What's the worst part about this?

- Why?

- Pulling out that wand again, what if you could get where you want to be and it was fun and easy?

- Let's create a plan to get you there. What are 3 small things that you would like to do this week to move you toward your goal?

    1.

    2.

    3.

Section 8: Quick Tips for Helping Teens Achieve Their Dreams

45. Dream Boards

Ages: 13-18

Purpose: To create a non-verbal modality of sharing goals. This exercise can be done at home as a family, individually, in the therapy office or in a group setting (if in a group setting, have the teens share their boards and say their dreams aloud).

Materials:

- Poster paper
- Glue stick
- Scissors
- Magazines
- Digital camera

Instructions:

Getting Started

- Instruct teens to start flipping through magazines looking for pictures, images or words that they love, are drawn to or light them up.
- Guide them a bit until they get the idea: What do you want in the next 6 months? What do you want to accomplish? What sport or activity do you want to try? (Keep the questions coming!)
- Cut out the pictures and set them aside.

Creating the Dream Board

- Take a photo of the teen, print it out and give it to them to paste in the center of the poster board.
- Take the pictures from the magazine and paste them to the board all around the photo.

Action Steps

- Tell the teen to place this dream board somewhere they will see it every day.
- Tell the teen to look at the board first thing in the morning and before bed.
- Check in with them from time to time and ask them if anything that they have put on their dream board has happened!

Section 8: Quick Tips for Helping Teens Achieve Their Dreams

46. Volunteering: Getting to Thank You!

Ages: All

Purpose: To give without getting something material or tangible in return. To teach empathy, the benefits of helping others, and how to make a difference. Kids who have issues are often called out on their negative behaviors. Here is a chance to allow them to feel appreciated and valued.

Therapists, parents, caregivers:

- Remember a time in your life when you volunteered or performed an act of service for another person or organization.

- Looking back, how did it feel?

- Now imagine that instead of volunteering you had been paid to do that work. How would that have changed the experience for you?

- What did you take away from your experience?

- If you are a therapist, how can you include volunteering or being of service to others in your treatment of children and families?

- If you are a parent/caregiver, what opportunities are there for your family to do something together for another person or organization?

Worksheet: Volunteering Brainstorm

Create a quick list of possible volunteering activities for the teen.

Say, "Let's brainstorm, I'll go first." Get silly, everything goes. See how many you can do in 10 minutes, set a timer!

1. _____
2. _____
3. _____
4. _____
5. _____
6. _____
7. _____
8. _____
9. _____
10. _____
11. _____
12. _____
13. _____
14. _____
15. _____
16. _____
17. _____
18. _____
19. _____
20. _____

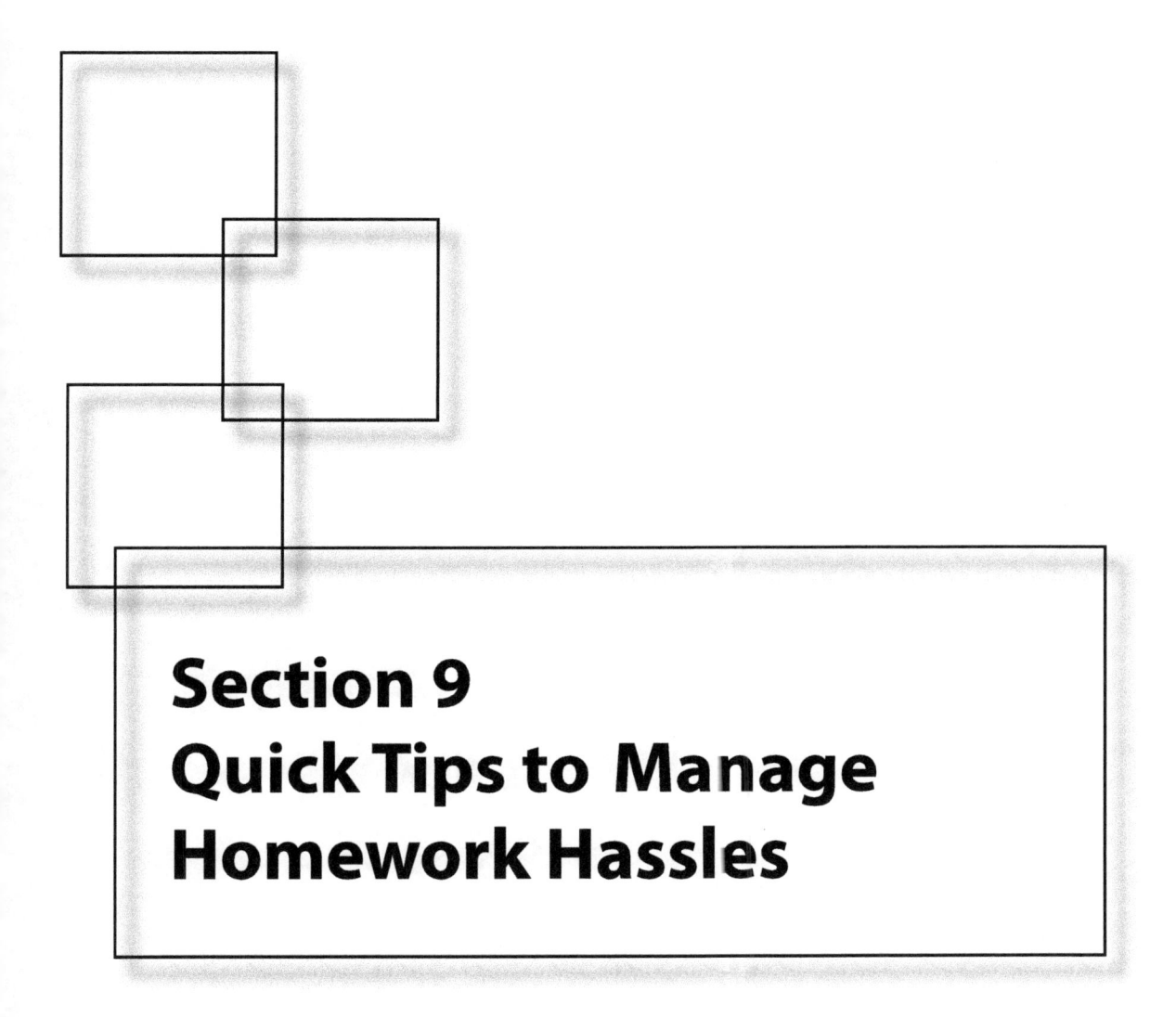

Section 9
Quick Tips to Manage Homework Hassles

Section 9: Quick Tips to Manage Homework Hassles

47. Setting Up a Homework Station

Ages: 5-18

Purpose: To provide a designated space for storing supplies and completing homework.

Materials:

- A specific area in your home (not their bedroom) where your child will not be distracted by TV or other things
- A credenza type desk or a tri-fold poster board to help block off distraction
- A white board or chalkboard: Set up the board where they can log in their home work and check off what they have done. This also helps when planning out long assignments. When your child comes home from school, have them write their assignments on the white board.
- School supplies: Pens, pencils, scissors, glue, tape, rulers, etc.
- Pockets or boxes for supplies

What this will teach your child:

- Self-discipline
- Organization
- Planning

What this will give you:

- Less stress and more free time for you!
- Remember, taking care of you is taking care of your kids.

Key Points for Parents:

- Get your child involved; take them shopping for supplies
- Buy supplies in advanced, have extras and things you may need for school projects
- If you have more than one child, make sure they each have their own homework station
- Make sure child is not slouching and not doing homework on the couch
- Inspect homework every day for completeness (if need be)

Section 9: Quick Tips to Manage Homework Hassles

48. We All Have Homework

Insist that homework is your child's responsibility and not yours. You don't need to sit down next to your child when they are doing their homework but you do need to be available (this means that you could be making dinner or you could be sitting with your laptop across from them doing your own work).

What to say:

"I am going to work while you work. We all have 'homework.'"

What Could Happen?

If your child says, "Mommy, I can't do it, I need your help," then go and sit next to your child and read the directions again with him out loud. Take one step at a time, have him do the problem and explain it to you out loud. Watch your child do the next problem by himself to make sure that he understood. If he gets stuck, go through the steps again and show your child how he can do it on his own. This way he will not be relying on you for every detail.

Section 9: Quick Tips to Manage Homework Hassles

49. Be a Helper, Not a Doer

Sometimes when we want to help our kids succeed we get carried away and end up doing their work for them. It is important to be clear with your children that you've already been to school and now it's their turn. When a child does something on their own with some help from you, they can feel really proud that they accomplished it. When you do it for them, at school they have to present the project or take the test and they are not going to do well because they have not integrated or understood the assignment because you did it for them. Make sure that you are a helper, not a doer.

Ways I can be a helper:

1. _____

2. _____

3. _____

4. _____

5. _____

Section 9: Quick Tips to Manage Homework Hassles

50. It's the Effort that Counts

Make sure you praise your child's efforts and not just the end product. Talk to our children about the path and the work that leads to goals.

Practice:

As your child is sitting there doing problem after problem, you want to be praising them on what a good job they are doing with sitting still, putting the pencil to paper and getting that homework done. Even when the going gets tough and they get frustrated, say:

- "I am really glad that you've been keeping at that one."

- "You can leave that problem, the one thats giving you a really hard time. We will come back to it later today but you are really working hard."

By praising their efforts, it encourages your child to do their homework the next time. If you tell them how smart they are, what are they going to do the next time to be smarter? Your child may feel like they have to live up to those expectations, which could lead to more stress and anxiety. Those kinds of compliments are passing and they feel good for you to say but do not help your child develop their own self-worth.

Section 9: Quick Tips to Manage Homework Hassles

51. Organize and Chunk Out Homework

Grouping assignments into similar chunks is very helpful for kids who have difficulty sticking with tasks and not getting distracted and for kids with shorter attention spans.

Materials:

- Timer

Instructions:

"We are going to do ten minutes of math and then we are going to take a break and then maybe we will do ten minutes of reading and then we'll take a break and then maybe we will go back and finish the math."

Important:

Take breaks. Set the timer in between assignments and play a game with your child (something quick: I Spy, Uno or tic-tac-toe).

Remember:

Keep them involved, chunk the time out depending on your child's age and their developmental stage and any issues they might be having with attention.

Section 9: Quick Tips to Manage Homework Hassles

52. Tutors and Mentors

You may consider getting a tutor if you're always battling with your child and don't want to be the bad guy anymore. So who could a tutor be? A tutor could be an older child in your neighborhood, a high school student, a middle school student if your child is younger, or an older cousin or even an older sibling if there is a good relationship there. Someone other than you!

Less stress for your child:

If you have a high school student and are having issues or if they suffer from ADD or anything like that, having a tutor can really take the edge off and help your teen feel successful. Having someone their own age or close to their age is also a way of role modeling for teens. If an older student tutors a younger student, your son or daughter may want to be a tutor to someone younger in return.

Section 9: Quick Tips to Manage Homework Hassles

53. Homework: When It's More Complex

Important for parents whose children have been diagnosed with ADHD, ADD, ODD, conduct disorder, obsessive-compulsive disorder, bipolar disorder, depression, anxiety, trauma, autism, etc.

Why am I still having problems?

Could it be lack of?

- structure
- system
- sleep
- nutrition
- respect
- too many electronics

When you try to get your child to do homework does s/he stick out his/her tongue?

Does s/he whine and complain?

Then replace it with:

A feasible system and good structure:

- Regular bedtime
- No TV in the bedroom
- Healthy diet
- Knowing your child's whereabouts

Kids diagnosed with ADD or another disability usually have learning disabilities as well. These learning disabilities include executive function disorder, auditory and visual processing disorder, dyslexia, dyscalculia, dysgraphia, dyspraxia, integration sequencing and distraction.

Challenging Children & Adolescents

Questions you should ask yourself about your child:

- Does your child have difficulty learning?
- Has your child been suspended from school?
- Has your child's teacher written on the report card, s/he is not working up to his/her potential? Or that your child appears "lazy"?
- Does your child have stomach aches or headaches a lot?
- Does your child not want to go to school?
- Does your child feel demoralized?
- Is your child already taking medication for ADHD, ADD, etc.?

If the house is chaotic and not running smoothly, you really need to go back to square one and try to get into a routine with:

- a regular dinnertime
- a regular bedtime
- removing the TV from the child's room
- making sure the food your child is getting is high in protein and low in sugar
- making sure that you are around or somebody is around when your child is getting their homework completed
- making sure that you are doing your mindful robotic parenting by letting them know that they cannot disrespect you

Use your words:

- Please don't speak to me that way.
- That's disrespectful.
- Model for your child how you want them to talk to you.

You can do it!

Implement your back to school program and instead of your child saying, "No I won't and you can't make me do my homework," your child will be saying, "Thanks so much for spending the time with me, for helping me get organized, for going to battle for me in school to make sure that I can get an education so that I can grow up and be a successful adult in this world."

Section 9: Quick Tips to Manage Homework Hassles

54. When's the Best Time to Do Homework?

Agree on specific times for doing the homework ahead of time and then stick to it. In our home, our kids came right home from school, got a snack and we pulled the homework stations up to the kitchen table. (I had a rolling cart with everything that they needed). After that we would have dinner. As the kids got older, they had to go back to their studies after dinner.

After school programs:

Now, you may have kids in sports and they stay after school, this may be a little more challenging for you. It is important that their homework gets done and they get to bed on time. Post the hours that homework will get done and stick to it (barring illness or other things when life happens to you).

Make an agreement with your child:

Write down your agreement. "We do homework between the hours of 4 and 6 p.m. in our house." Fill out the worksheet provided in this manual and hang it on the homework station or on the refrigerator. When your child says to you, "Mommy, can so and so come over?" You can say, "Well, we are not going to do that because our agreement is that homework gets done between 4 and 6." "Well mom, I finished my homework and its 4:30; now can my friend come over?" "Absolutely, you've done the homework first, now you can have a friend over or you can go out to play."

Remember:

- You are a helper, not a doer.

- Praise their efforts, not the end product or how smart they are.

- Insist that homework is your child's responsibility, not yours.

- Chunk out the homework into bite size pieces using a timer.

- Consider getting a tutor, if necessary.

- Agree on specific times for doing homework and post that agreement in a place where you both can see it.

Parent-Child Homework Agreement

Homework will begin at _____ and end at or before _____.

If homework is completed before _____ (time) _____ _____ (child/teen) _____ will be able to do the following activities:

1. _____

2. _____

3. _____

4. _____

5. _____

Child/Teen Signature _____

Parent/Caregiver Signature _____

Date _____

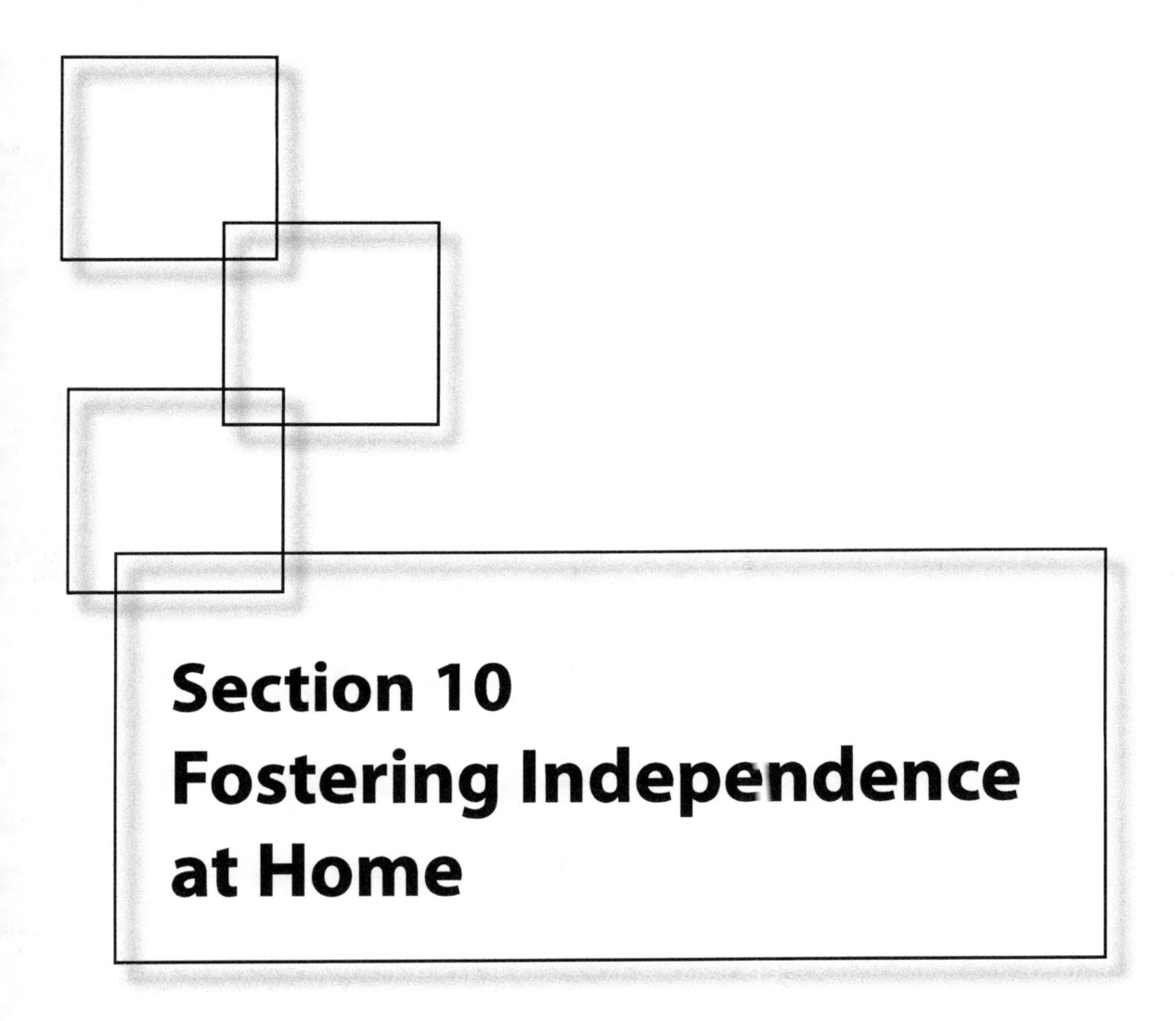

Section 10
Fostering Independence at Home

Section 10: Fostering Independence at Home

55. Which Behaviors Do You Want to Start or See More Of?

List what you want the child/teen to do. Fostering independence starts with identifying the "start" behaviors–behaviors we want to see more of.

Examples: Being on time for school, personal hygiene, completing homework, helping out around the house, etc.

1.

2.

3.

4.

5.

Section 10: Fostering Independence at Home

56. The Carrot and the Stick: Why Rewards Sometimes Don't Work

Rewards often don't work for getting kids to chip in around the house. Let me ask you, do you really blame your kids for not wanting to take out the trash, set the table, sweep the floor or clean up their rooms? Do you want to do it? Does paying them work in the long term? If you've tried the reward system, you know that it doesn't work forever.

Here are some tips to get your kids on board with helping out around the house:

- **Explain why doing the chore is necessary.** A chore that is not fun or interesting can become more meaningful if you can show your kids that it is part of the bigger picture. Explain that if each family member does one small chore each day you will have more time for the fun things your family gets to do, such as swimming or watching a movie together. Draw a picture of each person's contribution and show how your family is like a machine with all the moving parts helping the house run smoothly.

- **Say out loud: "Yes, I know that this chore is BORING."** Let your kids know that you understand that cleaning their room isn't a lot of fun. This isn't a lecture…it is empathy.

- **Let the kids do their chores their own way.** Don't control them. You can tell them that you want the table set, but you don't have to micro-manage where the fork and spoon go. Let them have fun and use their creative minds while doing their chore as long as it gets completed.

- **And if all else fails…use the Tom Sawyer method.** If you remember the story, Tom is white washing the fence and he is not having fun…but then he gets an idea. He tells his friend that painting the fence is not a grim chore, rather a fantastic privilege. His friend asks to try but Tom won't let him, saying it is way too fun. Finally, he gets his friend to give him an apple to try painting. Soon after, more boys arrive, and vie for the privilege of painting the fence. Pretend you are enjoying washing the dishes…make it look fun…soon your kids will be begging you to help.

Section 10: Fostering Independence at Home

57. How to Outsource Your Laundry for Free: Life Skills Training

Most parents struggle with getting kids to pitch in and do chores and most parents feel like all they do is nag the kids day in and day out. This can lead to explosive behaviors or parents doing everything for their kids to avoid conflict. Either way, a problem is created. Teaching personal responsibility is an essential component of parenting and raising successful children and young adults.

Parents have described their kid's room in the following ways: "A sea of clothing; wet, moldy towels; science experiments growing and not the type you get credit for!" "It is so horrifying that I would rather watch the latest Stephen King film than open the door to my son's room." "And to top it off, I have to beg, threaten and coerce to get my kids to hand over their dirty clothing so that I can wash it. Once I give it back, neatly folded, stacked and clean they don't even put it away!"

Ages: 9-18

Purpose: To teach independent living skills, appreciation for one's belongings and to reduce parent-child conflict.

Instructions:

- Purchase two laundry baskets for each child: one white and one other color and place inside their rooms.
- Write out easy to understand instructions for your washer and dryer and tape them to the front of your machines.
- Have a field trip with your kids to the laundry room.
- Explain to your kids that they will be in charge of their own laundry from now on, including their towels and sheets.
- Give a laundry lesson and tell your kids that as they undress, the whites go in the white basket and everything else into the other basket.
- Assign your kids 1 or 2 days each week that they will 'get to' use the machines.
- Inform them that if they don't transfer their clothing from one machine to the other or remove their clothing from the dryer that they risk having it dumped on the floor by the next person in line to wash clothes.

Challenging Children & Adolescents

- Do not bail your child out. Let them forget, let them find their clothing on the floor, wet and smelly.
- You are teaching independence, accountability, respect and consideration for others. You are also teaching that all the household chores should not fall on one person (YOU). You are giving your children a gift for life. And at the same time, you get to stop nagging, you get free time and it didn't cost you a penny!

Section 10: Fostering Independence at Home

58. Kids as Cooks

Ages: 3-18

Purpose: To teach children life skills for independence, create family time, make chores fun, streamline the home.

Materials:

- Bread for enough sandwiches to feed the kids lunch for one week
- Luncheon meats, tuna fish, PB&J, or whatever else you and the kids like
- Labels or scraps of paper for labeling
- Sandwich bags or tin foil, whatever you prefer

Instructions:

- On Sunday afternoon, set up an assembly line at the kitchen table.
- Have the kids lay out all the bread on cookie sheets or parchment paper on the kitchen table.
- Also have piles of lunch meats, condiments, peanut butter and jelly. Have the kids make all the sandwiches.
- Have the kids label them.
- Put the sandwiches in your freezer where the kids can see the labels. (If you have a deep freeze with a top rack, or your fridge has a bottom freezer this works best for kids to be able to see and reach.)
- In the fridge or on the counter, have a fruit bowl available where the kids can grab an apple, orange, banana, etc.
- In the cabinet or on the counter, have a dessert/snack dish available with portion size snacks available to add to the lunches. (Pre-measure the snacks—raisins, cookies, crackers, cheese—into snack size sandwich bags. Kids can also do this and it is cheaper than buying them already snack-sized.)
- In the morning before sitting down to breakfast, have the kids choose a sandwich from the freezer, a piece of fruit, a snack, dessert, napkin, etc. (If they go to day camp or daycare have them put the items in the lunch box. If you do this in August, getting ready to return to school will be a breeze!)
- You should also do the same for yourself— think of all the money you will save by not eating out for lunch!

Section 10: Fostering Independence at Home

59. Magic Black Bag: How Not to Trip Over Backpacks, Skateboards, Etc.

Ages: 5-18

Purpose: To create organization at home, reduce parent/child conflict.

Instructions:

- Tell your child/teen that by a certain time, 9pm for example, clothes, belongings, etc. must be off the floor and out of your sight.

- At 8:30pm give the first reminder.

- At 9pm collect everything that was not picked up.

- Take this bag and hide it in the back of a closet or lock it in the trunk of your car.

- Tell the teen that they will not get these things back until 3 days have passed with nothing that you have tripped on.

- Stick to it and don't cave. Believe me, by the next night they will be rushing to get their things before you do.

- The key is consistency, scheduling and following through.

- Natural consequences are terrific. If the Algebra book ends up in the bag and your teen has to explain to the teacher what happened, most teachers will back you up since they are trying to teach these same skills in the classroom.

Section 10: Fostering Independence at Home

60. Allowance is What You Are Allowed: Early Lessons in Financial Responsibility

Children are exposed to more and more "stuff" every day so of course, they want more and more. Parents are frazzled because they feel like they are spoiling their children and worry about their futures. Most parents these days have incurred some type of debt like credit card, student loans, mortgage, etc. so they understand what it means to "**OWE**."

Ages: 5-14

Purpose: To teach children the consequences of making poor financial decisions and mismanaging their money early on when the consequences are not as severe.

How to:

1. Each child is allotted 3-5 envelopes (depending on the age, stage and needs of the child).
2. Each envelope is labeled with something like:

    - **Spending Money $1.50** (little things, gum, candy, little toy, etc.)
    - **Lunch Money $5.00** (to bring to school)
    - **Bank Deposit Money $2.00** (College fund, saving for first car–something BIG and long term. Open up a children's savings account and let your child watch the money grow and the interest accumulate. Kids love this!)
    - **Something I am saving for $1.50** (Something your child is asking for that is a bit bigger–new video game, toy, etc.)
    - **Charity $1.00** (church, synagogue or charity of child's choice)

3. Decide how much you want your child to put in each envelope.
4. Pick one day a week (like Sunday morning) to divide up the allowance.
5. Make sure you have $1s and change.
6. Hand your child the money and have them divide it up and put it in the correct envelopes.
7. Now for the fun part! Before you go to the store, tell your children if they want to buy anything they need to bring along their "Spending Money" envelope.

8. When you get to the store, do not get involved with the purchase. Let them decide how to spend their money.
9. If they ask to borrow from one envelope to put more in another envelope, let them but have them write an **IOU** to that envelope. Tell them that until the **IOU** is paid up each week's "spending money" has to go to the other envelope.
10. Let them feel their successes and their failures; this is a wonderful lesson to give your kids!

Section 10: Fostering Independence at Home

61. Just One More Glass of Water: Getting Kids to Bed and Sleeping Through the Night

Do you dread bedtime? Does your child call to you after you have already read 3 stories, checked for monsters, lined up the stuffed animals and made sure that the door was ajar in exactly the correct position to your child's specifications? Does your child get out of bed over and over until you are both exhausted and your child is crying?

Does your child demand that you lie down with her/him? And stay there until s/he falls asleep? Do you find yourself drifting off and waking up two hours later in your child's bed? Or worse, when you try to sneak out, does your child wake up and demand that you return? Or do you wake up in your own bed and notice the extra little body sleeping peaceful beside you?

If any of this sounds familiar, then you are probably waking up exhausted in the morning, dragging yourself through your day and dreading the evening when it all starts again. How would you like to be able to tuck your child into bed with a nighttime kiss and have the rest of the night for you? How would you like to wake up feeling rested and refreshed the next morning? Would you like to have enough energy to make it through your day without needing a nap and actually look forward to bedtime with your child?

Ages: 3-9

Purpose: To create safety at bedtime and increase the amount of time children stay in their own beds. (Also to restore parents by getting the sleep they need!)

Instructions:

- Remove the TV from your child's bedroom.
- Buy a portable timer.
- Buy or make a special pillow or stuffed toy.

Challenging Children & Adolescents

Tonight:

- Before dinner, tell your child that there will be a new bedtime plan. Give them the pillow or stuffed animal and tell them that this is their very own Magical Protector. It keeps monsters out of kid's rooms, helps kids get comfy and fall asleep very fast.
- 10 minutes before bedtime, tell your child they get to choose 2 to 3 stories, but no more. After you read each story repeat, "Ok that was story number __, we have __ left."
- Tuck your child in. Tell the child that you have a timer and are going to set the timer to go off in 5 minutes and that you will return to make sure that the Magical Protector is doing its job.
- When you go back, reassure your child that s/he is safe and tell them you will be back again in 6 minutes. Keep going back with longer intervals in between checks.
- If your child gets out of bed, calmly walk him/her back to bed and repeat from the beginning of the timed checks.
- If your child ends up in your bed, repeat the drill. I know you are tired, do it anyway!

The average time it takes to retrain your child is about 3 days (sometimes more and sometimes less). The less you give in, the quicker your success will be and the more rested and peaceful you will feel!

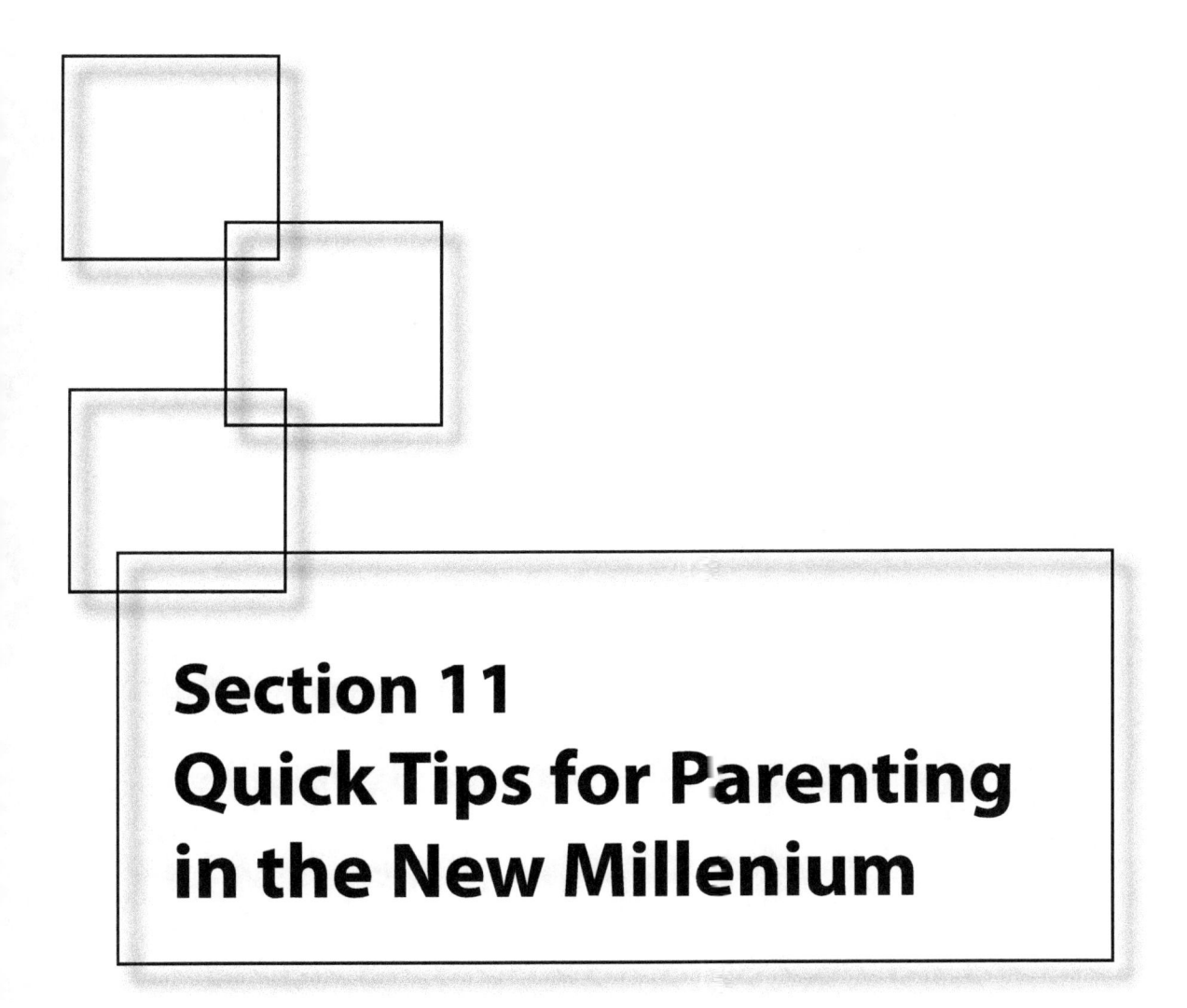

Section 11
Quick Tips for Parenting in the New Millenium

Section 11: Quick Tips for Parenting in the New Millenium

62. Blended Families and Discipline: "You're not my dad! You can't tell me what to do!"

Second marriages and adult unions bring up issues for kids. You may have noticed that the kids are acting out or retreating to their rooms more often. It is a good idea for you and your future spouse to decide how you will handle discipline before you live together or marry. No matter if you are a new stepparent or you have been hitting your head against the wall for what seems like years trying to get peace at home, take a deep breath and try these 5 steps.

Step #1: Step-parent as Uncle/Aunt, Friend, Coach, etc.

As a new stepparent, you have your job cut out for you. In the beginning, take a step back and see yourself as needing to connect with the kids rather than disciplining them. Let the teenager's biological parent handle the correcting, reprimanding, etc. Work on creating a close relationship with the new teen in your life. Do this until the teen has accepted you. Even if you have been blended for years, take a step back.

Step # 2: Stay Neutral

Don't get pulled into a debate between your spouse and their child/teen about a behavior. Let your spouse handle the situation. Only join in when/if your spouse asks for your help.

Step #3: Get a Hobby

Allow your spouse/partner to have "alone/special" time with their child/teen. The kids need this and your marital relationship needs this, too. There is plenty of time for family time. Let the kids know that you are not taking their mom or dad away from them.

Step #4: Offer Help

Offer your help to the child/teen in areas of homework, sports, problem solving. Even if they turn you down, don't retreat. Let the kids know that you are available if they have a problem or need help.

Step #5: Family Meeting

Once you have bonded with the children you can begin sharing some of the discipline with your spouse. With your spouse, set up a few house rules and consequences and share these with the kids during your family meeting. This takes you out of the middle. It also makes you and your spouse a united front.

Section 11: Quick Tips for Parenting in the New Millenium

63. Sleep and Obesity: What's the Connection?

Children under 5 who do not get at least 10 hours of sleep at night are almost twice as likely to be overweight or obese later in childhood, a new study reports. And naps during the day don't count.

A study, published {September 6, 2010} in *Archives of Pediatrics & Adolescent Medicine*, analyzed data from a nationally representative sample of 1,930 children under 14. The data included detailed diaries from two random days, in whichparents recorded the amount of time a child spent in various activities, among them sleeping.

The study adds to an existing body of evidence suggesting that sleep plays an important role in weight regulation, perhaps because tired children are not as active or because sleep affects hormones that influence hunger and appetite, said the paper's lead author, Janice F. Bell, an assistant professor at the University of Washington School of Public Health in Seattle.

"What we're saying is that adequate sleep at age 0 to 5 is probably more important than we think," Dr. Bell said, adding that the good news is that "it's a modifiable risk factor — it's something we can change."

- Roni Caryn Rabin (New York Times, September 2010)

So, how do we get kids to sleep more?

Think back to your own childhood...how much time did you spend outdoors?

I grew up in the sixties in New England. The winters were BRRRR and the springs were very rainy. We played for hours in the snow without waterproof mittens either. I still remember banging on the door asking for a dry pair because the pair I was wearing was completely frozen with icicles hanging off!

By the age of 10, I had my own paper route. The papers were delivered at 4:30PM, 7 days a week 365 days a year. I did this for 4 years on foot. I saved every penny, banked it and made a whopping $400! And guess what, I walked the route in all kinds of weather.

My point is, the outdoors were a huge part of my universe, which was good for me and good for my mom. (She got things done and got a break from the kids!)

Challenging Children & Adolescents

But, sadly, the world has changed and parents are afraid to let children roam unsupervised. "They might get snatched!" Or maybe your neighbors will judge you, "That parent doesn't supervise her children!"

In 2005, the manufacturers of Persil® washing powder did a survey called "Dirt is good: The 33 things you should do before you're 10."

Here are some of them: (Have you done these things? Have your kids?)

- Roll down a grassy bank
- Make a mud pie
- Catch frogs
- Build a sandcastle
- Climb a tree
- Make snow angels
- Take part in a scavenger hunt
- Camp out in the yard
- Feed a farm animal
- Find some worms
- Ride a bike through a mud puddle
- Make and fly a kite
- Find ten different leaves
- Plant a tree

These activities don't cost a cent, provide plenty of fresh air and tire kids out, which helps kids sleep for more hours. According to studies, kids who sleep more are less likely to have a weight problem. This is a wonderful start to a full, active, healthy life that you can provide for your children.

Section 11: Quick Tips for Parenting in the New Millenium

64. Healthy Home Makeover

Technology has made so much of what we do faster, more convenient and much more streamlined. I remember the days of typewriters, Wite-Out® and spending an entire day typing a one page paper only to make a mistake in the last paragraph! The mess of the Wite-Out® and the typewriter ribbon and having to do it again and again! As I write this chapter, I can change my mind and make a mistake without a mess and be done in a fraction of the time it took thirty years ago.

We no longer have to get out of our cars, let alone out of our homes to shop thanks to the internet, certainly convenient! We can use the drive-thru at the pharmacy, restaurant, library, bank and even some post-offices. But convenience has its price. We are a society that has become sedentary—nearly everything we want is at our fingertips.

We are getting fatter and sicker in the U.S. According to Dr. Lawrence J. Cheskin at Johns Hopkins University:

- In the USA, excess weight, obesity and inactivity are responsible for about 300,000 deaths each year.
- Complications from obesity may increase the risk of: heart attacks, type 2 diabetes, stroke, osteoarthritis, and certain cancers
- Surveys show that at least 66 percent of American adults are overweight or obese and the percentage of overweight or obese children has doubled over the past 30 years to 25 percent of the under 19 population.
- Did you know that adults make at least 200 food choices every day?
- Overweight kids get picked on and bullied. This leads to depression and eating disorders.

Things you can do to get your kids and family on track:

1. Breakfast—Start the day off right

2. Exercise—Get out of the car, skip the drive-thru, take the stairs instead of the elevator— MOVE!

3. Teamwork—Support each other, don't sabotage your healthy home.

4. Eat low fat meals 6 times a day—Plan, plan, plan. Cook healthy on the weekends, divide and freeze.

5. Know your metabolism—Be conscious and tuned into your body. Know how many calories it takes to keep you at your optimal weight.

6. Weigh yourself weekly—Catch little weight gains and adjust your calorie intake accordingly.

Section 11: Quick Tips for Parenting in the New Millenium

65. Technology and Distractibility: Its Affect on Concentration

Going back to school is one of those transitions that happens every year. Parents start rolling back bedtimes, practice getting kids to bed earlier and up in the morning earlier, too. Shopping for new shoes, uniforms, backpacks, notebooks, binders, pencils are part of the new school year ritual as well. In the past several years with the advent of cell phones, mp3 players and laptops, it has come to the attention of school personnel, parents and other professionals that while technology is a wonderful thing, it can also be a huge distraction for students.

When I looked up the definition of "multitasking," this is what I found: *The concurrent operation by one central processing unit of two or more processes.* The definition came about in the 1960's to describe computer or CPU capabilities. Computers don't have feelings, emotions or concentration, so multitasking can be a very smooth process. There are no obstacles except possibly a poorly written algorithm. People, on the other hand, do have feelings, emotions and require concentration to get most jobs done.

Within the last 5 years or so technology has seen an even bigger boom than most of us could ever have imagined. Just as we were amazed at an astronaut landing on the moon in 1968, we baby boomers are blown away by computers, cell phones and Twitter.

The impact of technology on children, tweens and teens is astounding. Kids now-a-days seem to breathe text messaging. No longer are kids giving out the home telephone number; in fact, many families don't even have a landline.

Some of this is good because we can contact our kids at will, but some aspects of this are also troubling:

- Looking at their phones hundreds of times a day–interrupted thought process
- Conversations being interrupted to respond to a text message–not finishing sentences
- Sleeping with phones–interrupted sleep
- Phones at school–interruptions in class
- Phones during homework–interrupted concentration

Challenging Children & Adolescents

An article in USA Today in August 2009, referred to a phenomenon called "Cultural Autism" with the use of cell phones and computer communication, which led to:

- Inability to express feelings or emotions face to face
- Fear of using telephones to set up their own appointments
- Inability to have face to face conversations.

Some solutions to this problem for you to consider this school year:

- Before you purchase your child's first cell phone, ask yourself, "Why am I doing this?" If it is because your child is begging you saying that s/he cannot live without it and everyone else has one, think good and hard before you buy.

- Decide if your child/tween/teen really requires his or her cell phone while at school and if not, do not allow them to bring it.

- Cell phones are handed over to parents after school and returned when homework is completed.

- Cell phones are handed over to parents during the child's sleeping hours.

- Cell phones will become a power struggle. There is no way around it. Having a system for controlling their use will ensure that your child grows up socially adept and with a mind that can focus on one thing at a time.

Cell phones are only one distraction and there are many more. Before your child/tween/teen starts school take a look at the computer, DS, Wii, TV, etc. What do you need to do to help limit these distractions? And while you are at it, look at all of this for you as well.

Section 11: Quick Tips for Parenting in the New Millenium

66. Enjoying Your Kids While Working from Home

More and more parents are choosing to work from home which is great news because kids have more access to their parents. However, working from home while raising a family can present challenges that are difficult to handle, such as:

- Setting limits
- Being interrupted
- Balancing work with family life

Instructions:

1. Make a schedule and stick to it. Whether you work days, afternoons or evenings let your family know your hours. You might hang your schedule in the kitchen or on the door to your office. If you must work while your children are home (after school) arrange for a school aged babysitter to come over to play with the kids a couple of times a week.

2. At the end of your workday, turn off your computer, clean your desk and make a to-do list for tomorrow. Do not answer your work phone or emails after you have closed shop. If you were at the office, you wouldn't know about these messages until the following morning. These small steps help you to walk away and enjoy time with your family.

3. If your office also doubles as family space, create boundaries for your papers and files. If the kids are going to use your "work" computer for homework and surfing, teach them to create folders so everyone's documents have a place to be stored. Give the kids clear instructions about what is acceptable to download. This will eliminate you nagging the kids to get off the computer and you can have more pleasant interactions with your family.

4. Install a separate phone line dedicated solely to your business. This will keep unwanted interruptions from happening and a clear line of communication open for you and your business. Back to the computer; if you can afford to, have another computer for the family.

Challenging Children & Adolescents

5. Enlist your school age children to help with office tasks that they can handle such as stamping envelopes, creating a data base or shredding unwanted documents. If you compensate the kids (with either a reward such as time with you or payment), they will want to pitch in. You will also be teaching them how important your work is to all your lives.

6. If possible, create other work spaces in your office, where your children can do homework and projects while you catch up on your own work. This allows you to spend time with your children while working.

You have made the choice to work from home and your children are fortunate to have you around. Make your time with your kids fun and look for new and creative ways to allow the kids to participate in your business, thereby increasing time they are spending with you.

Section 11: Quick Tips for Parenting in the New Millenium

67. Family Meetings: Run Your Home Like a Business

Is it difficult to get your family together? Are meal times chaotic? Are you stuck doing all the chores? Is your family operating individually and not as a team? Do members of your family have constant miscommunications? Is your teenager disengaged from the family, isolating in his or her room, always at a friend's house, never home or never available? If so, do you want to increase communication, have everyone be on the same page and plan fun and enjoyable times together?

Then read on…
A family meeting is a great way to improve communication with your teenager and have an organized, enjoyable and meaningful family life.

What exactly is a family meeting?
A family meeting provides you the forum to pull your family together, communicate the week's events/responsibilities and make family decisions about household chores or even planning a vacation!

How to Set Up Your First Family Meeting

- Pick a time and place (e.g. the living room on Sunday morning at 11am)
- Tell your family that this meeting will be no longer than 30 minutes.
- At the start of the first meeting ask someone in the family to volunteer to take notes and someone to watch the clock.
- Let family members know that everyone will be taking turns with note taking and running the meetings.
- Let them know that this meeting is mandatory (important decisions will be made; if they don't show, then they won't have a say).

Challenging Children & Adolescents

Sample Agenda for Your First Family Meeting

1. Introduce the concept of the family meeting (why do you want to have family meetings?)
    a. Set a time: Meetings will be held every Sunday at 11am for no longer than 30 minutes.
    b. Everyone is expected to be there.
    c. If a member cannot be there, explain that the meeting notes will be kept in a notebook available for all family members to review.

2. Establish rules and procedures for the meetings
    a. One person talks at a time.
    b. All suggestions are welcome.
    c. No judgment; no one gets to be wrong.

3. Explain that a blank agenda will be posted on the fridge where family members can fill in topics to be discussed at the next meeting.

4. Come up with something fun to do after the meeting and do it.

A family meeting does not work if:

- they are held at the dinner table or in the car
- kids complain or whine
- parents use the meetings to discipline

How to have the best family meeting on the block:

- Start the meeting with compliments.
    - Tell your children all the great things that you noticed about them in the past week.
    - Even if you are at a loss, find something positive to say anyway!
    - Ask the teens to say positive things to the other family members and so forth.
- During the meeting make sure that everyone gets to say how they feel.
- Make sure you reach a resolution during the discussion.
- Record and document your family meetings and keep the notes available to everyone.
- At the beginning of the next meeting, review the notes from the previous meeting.
- **Always end with something fun which helps family members feel good, like a group hug, game or family ritual.**

Section 11: Quick Tips for Parenting in the New Millenium

68. How to Write a Family Mission Statement

Ages: 4-18

Purpose: To help foster communication, peace and harmony at home. To help teach children/teens accountability, planning and organizational skills.

Instructions:

- Start with a family meeting.
- Explain that by having a family mission statement there will be less confusion about what your day to day and long term goals as a family are.
- Get the kids to talk about what makes your family special and take notes. (For instance: we are funny, we like to go camping, we like to go to the movies, we like celebrating, volunteering, etc.)
- Now come up with sentences that reflect those values that are within the specialness of the family.

"The Jones family loves to spend time together whether we are celebrating birthdays or just eating dinner together. We love to make each other laugh and are respectful to one another and strive to be considerate at all times. We understand that we all make mistakes and that we can learn from these; therefore, we take responsibility for our own actions. We believe that it is important to be involved in our community and help others who are less fortunate."

- Continue to edit the statement until the family is in agreement and all members feel that they had a part in its creation.
- Print out the mission statement, frame it and hang it in a place for all to see.
- When family members notice that the family is drifting from the values, suggest that the family members re-read the statement.
- Once or twice a year have a special family meeting to go over the mission statement and update accordingly.

Worksheet: Family Mission Statement

"We the _____ family, love to _____

_____

We value_____

_____

We understand_____

_____

We believe_____

_____."

Bibliography

Barkley, Russell A. (1997). *Defiant children: a clinician's manual for assessment and parent training*. New York: The Guilford Press.

Bronson, P., & Merryman, A. (2009). *Nurtureshock: new thinking about children*. New York: Twelve.

Crawford, C. (2009). *The highly intuitive child: a guide to understanding and parenting unusually sensitive and empathic children*. Alameda, CA: Hunter House Inc.

Epstein, S. & Rosenkrantz, D. (2010). *Your out of control teen: the little book with a lot of attitude: a guide to effective parent-teen communication*. Shining Star Publishing.

Epstein, S. (2008). *Are you tired of nagging? get your kids to cooperate: how to raise well-behaved children*. Shining Star Publishing.

Epstein, S. (2007). *Taking back your parenting power system: how to get control of your kids in 30 days or less: the secret formula to powerful parenting*. Shining Star Publishing.

Ginsburg, K. R. (2006). *A parent's guide to building resilience in children and teens: giving your child roots and wings*. Elk Grove Village, IL: American Academy of Pediatrics.

Ginsburg, K. R. (2002). *"But I'm almost 13!": an action plan for raising a responsible adolescent*. New York: Contemporary Books.

Glasser, W. (1998). *Choice Theory: a new psychology of personal freedom*. New York: HarperCollins Publishers, Inc.

Greene, R. W. & Ablon, J. S. (2006). *Treating explosive kids: the collaborative problem-solving approach*. New York: The Guilford Press.

James, B. (1989). *Treating traumatized children: new insights and creative interventions*. New York: The Free Press.

Kindlon, D., & Thompson, M. (1999). *Raising cain: protecting the emotional life of boys*. New York: Ballantine Books.

Minuchin, S. (1974). *Families and family therapy*. Cambridge, MA: Harvard University Press.

Minuchin, S., & Fishman, H.C. (2002). *Family therapy techniques*. Cambridge, MA: Harvard University Press.

Palmer, S. (2006). *Toxic childhood: how the modern world is damaging our children and what we can do about it*. Great Britain: Orion.

Pink, D. H. (2009). *Drive: the surprising truth about what motivates us.* Riverhead Books.

Rappaport, L. (2009). *Focusing-oriented art therapy: Accessing the body's wisdom and creative intelligence.* London: Jessica Kingsley Publishers.

Szapocznik, J., Hervis, O. E., & Schwartz, S. J. (2003). Brief Strategic Family Therapy for Adolescent Drug Abuse (NIH Pub. No. 03–4751). *NIDA Therapy Manuals for Drug Addiction*, Manual 5. Rockville, MD: National Institute on Drug Abuse.

Taibbi, R. (2007). *Doing family therapy: craft and creativity in clinical practice, second edition.* New York: The Guilford Press.

Whitworth, L., Kimsey-House, H., & Sandahl, P. (1998). *Co-active coaching: new skills for coaching people toward success in work and life.* Mountain View, CA: Davies-Black Publishing.

Additional Resources on the Web

www.ParentingPowers.com
Susan P. Epstein, LCSW, free special reports and free weekly tele-classes for parents on a wide variety of parenting topics

www.freebehaviorcharts.com
Mona Grayson

partnersforrecovery.samhsa.gov/rosc.html
Partners for Recovery (PFR) addresses issues of national significance and it is driven by the individual, families and communities it serves. The PFR Initiative supports and provides technical resources to those who deliver services for the prevention and treatment of substance use conditions and co-occurring mental health and seeks to build capacity and improve services and systems of care.

www.nami.org
National Alliance on Mental Illness

www.ffcmh.org
National Federation of Families for Children's Mental Health

www.spectrummentor.com
Brian King, "Beyond social skills…strategies for building meaningful relationships for people on the Autism Spectrum…"

www.Effects-of-Marijuana.com